álvaro castells

internet dictionary

a comprehensive guide to the language of the Web

First published in Spain in 2000 by Ediciones Deusto, S A, Alameda Recalde 27, 48009 Bilbao, Spain
First published the UK by Kogan Page, 2002

Kogan Page Limited
120 Pentonville Road
London N1 9JN
UK

Kogan Page US
22 Broad Street
Milford CT 06460
USA

British Library Cataloguing in Publication Data

A CIP record for this book is available from the British Library.

ISBN 0 7494 3667 0

Editorial staff:
Direction: Joaquín Navarro
Coordination: Josep Dávila
Edition: Catriona Watson-Brown, Javier Pérez Andujar
Design: Joan Pejoan
Layout: Núria Lombarte
Translation: Guido Castañeda Macchiavello, Francis Linn, Mauricio Schwarz, Sandra Young

Printed and bound in Great Britain by Biddles Ltd, Guildford and King's Lynn
www.biddles.co.uk

FOREWORD

In his preface to The Critique of Practical Reason, *Immanuel Kant wrote:*

> *I have no fear, as regards this treatise, of the reproach that I wish to introduce a new language, since the sort of knowledge here in question has itself somewhat of an everyday character... I am more afraid in the present treatise of occasional misconception in respect of some expressions that I have chosen with the greatest care in order that the notion to which they point may not be missed.*

These words of the renowned German philosopher struck me as being applicable to the excellent work of Álvaro Castells in this book. I believe that Álvaro has been able to gather in this dictionary a truly new language, which is increasing in popularity on a daily basis. The depth and breadth of his writing and the carefully drafted definitions are features that set this work apart from others in this field.

All forecasts accept the Internet as an essential and unstoppable tool for the immediate future of both public and business communications. This should not come as a surprise: the sheer speed at which the Internet has gained a stronghold on our society should make us aware of its importance. In the United States, it took 40 years for electricity to be present in just 30 per cent of homes; telephone took 35 years to become widely established and radio 25 years. To attain the same degree of penetration, the Internet took just 5 years. We all agree upon the revolutionary changes brought about by the development of electricity, telephone, radio and television – the full implications of the Internet revolution are still to come.

The Internet has driven society to a new age full of expectation, opportunity, risk and, yes, confusion. If you do not understand what is going on in this relatively early stage of the Internet revolution, you will face serious difficulties in getting to grips with this new world later on.

The speculative hype of the late nineties and the growth of the Nasdaq has given way to caution regarding e-business, with some so-called 'gurus' going so far as to predict the end of the new economy, but I believe that we are standing at the threshold of a change that will radically transform our lives. We know how, where and when Internet began, but nobody knows how far or in which direction it will lead us.

In the business world, the Internet has given rise to an interesting phenomenon; generally speaking, companies for which I have worked in the past followed a process whereby they first developed a product or service, then struggled to work out the best channel to reach the user or customer. The Internet has turned this whole process upside down – there is a readily available network where you can sell infinite varieties of products and services to a multitude of customers, worldwide.

This tidal wave of new products and services has had a deep impact on the company that I now lead, Telefonica. As well as transforming its business practices, the Internet is transforming the very business of Telefonica, which is responding to the substantial increase in data traffic over voice traffic.

I believe that the initiative of Álvaro Castells has created a useful book that helps us to understand in an accessible and friendly way the terminology used in the ongoing Internet revolution. I recommend that anyone wanting to get to grips with the Internet environment should have handy a copy of The Internet Dictionary.

Cesar Alierta
President, Telefonica

PREFACE

In 1995, I began to use the Internet as a work tool to make it easier to locate specific information on books and articles that I was writing at that time. Scarcely realising, I rapidly entered into a different world. A world in which the rules of behaviour of the people involved in it were different to those of the real world. In this new world, a language was being created at lightning speed. New words to describe things that did not exist or for renaming the old things. Combinations of symbols representing emotions, or acronyms that were used in chat rooms. Without realising, that new language became an extension of my habitual language. Five years later, that language has come into every-day use. We can see new words being used in the media, in advertising or in any conversation between friends or professionals. However, when I am preparing an article or a conference, I usually have to give special attention to the words I use, as there are very few that have been extended into general use.

Since 1997, I have been taking special note of all those new words that have appeared. Words that people around me often ask, or words I read in documents about the Internet, or those that I hear at conferences, etc. The result of these last four years almost, is the book you have in your hands. A compendium of nearly one thousand words, written in airport lounges, on aeroplanes, trains, the Luarca library (in Asturias), and especially during many nights and weekends at home, taking away hours of dedication to Sandra and Rodrigo. But with the illusion of creating something useful.

I would also like to thank Erika Vallespin and Rafael Ardit who were enthusiastic about the project from the very start and supported me throughout.

A dictionary is something alive, and this dictionary shouldn't be any different. New words are continually cropping up. Words that will require new, revised editions. But, without a doubt, you will always be able to find the meaning of the more widely-used words in this copy.

Álvaro Castells

NUMBERS

64k Line
Digital telephone connection capable of transmitting 64,000 bps (bits per second).

128 encryption
A maximum-security cipher system, initially used in the United States for military purposes. It is mainly used in Europe by banking institutions, although it has more recently become available to other enterprises, such as the Spanish National Currency and Stamp Factory, which in 1999 used it to receive income tax statements over the Internet.

404, 404 not found, error 404
A number which corresponds to a fairly common error message on the Internet; '404 Not Found' indicates that the *URL* requested cannot be located, either because the page no longer exists or because its server is offline. It appears in the browser as a web page.

SIGNS

:-)
See SMILEY

@, at, at sign, address sign
The @ symbol (read as 'at', 'at sign' or 'address sign') is most commonly used in e-mail addresses, where it separates the user's name or identification from the address, such as in alvaro@atkearney.com.

@Home

An enterprise resulting from the merger of Excite Inc. and @Home Network. @Home has reached an agreement with the most important US and Canadian ca-

ble companies to offer high-speed access for a monthly fee. Cable affords a much higher Internet download speed than the standard telephone connection. It offers huge advantages for downloading online music and video, participating in multiplayer games on the Internet, or watching movies. @Home uses its own browser based on Microsoft Internet Explorer. It can be visited at www.home.com
See @WORK

@Work
Excite's @Home services for companies. Its website is at www.work.home.net
See @HOME

Abilene
The name of the *backbone* of Internet2. Both are the main projects of US-based UCAID (University Corporation for Advanced Internet Development).
See INTERNET2

.ac
The extension (taken from 'academy') used for domains linked to educational institutions, such as universities, high schools, academies and colleges. It is usually followed by the country domain name, which indicates the location of the educational centre, such as Oxford University (www.ox.ac.uk) or Tokyo University (www.u-tokyo.ac.jp). The '.edu' extension is more widely used in the United States and does not require a country domain name.
See DOMAINS

Acceptable User Policy
See AUP

access
This can have several meanings. The most usual denotes connection to the Internet (Internet access). It can also mean the type of connection (network, dial-up, cable modem, etc.) or the possibility of visiting a pay-as-you-go website or one requiring registration for authorised entry.

access number
The telephone number used to connect to an *ISP (Internet Service Provider)*.

access privileges
Permission to read and/or modify files on a network.

access provider
See ISP (INTERNET SERVICE PROVIDER)

ACK (acknowledge)
1 Used to acknowledge a user's presence in the network; it is the appropriate answer to a *ping*.
2 When one computer sends a block of data to another through a network, the second computer sends back an ACK return message to indicate the transfer has been successful, i.e. the data block has reached its destination without errors. If errors are detected in the transmission, the second computer can return a negative ACK (*NAK*).
See PING, XMODEM

Acrobat

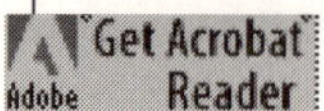

One of the most widely used programs on the Internet, although it was originally a multimedia and graphics application. Adobe developed the Acrobat software to create, save and view documents in *PDF (Portable Document Format)* whilst keeping the same appearance as the originals. The files can then be read using Acrobat Reader, a piece of software that can be downloaded free of charge from the Adobe website (www.adobe.com) or from

multiple links on the Internet. One of Acrobat's main advantages is that it allows very large documents to be saved as much smaller files, making them ideal for rapid transfer via the Internet and for storage on hard disks with low memory capacity. Acrobat can be used in tandem with an Internet browser, or even as a *plug-in*, enabling documents to be opened from within the browser.
See PDF

Acrobat Reader
See Acrobat

acronym
From the Greek, meaning 'extremity' and 'name'. In the context of the Internet and computing in general, it describes the abbreviated form of a frequently used phrase, created by using the initials of the individual words. Acronyms are most commonly used in *chat rooms* and, to a lesser extent, in e-mail and *newsgroups*, etc. They are always written in capital letters. Some of the best known are:

AND	Any Day Now
AFAIK	As Far As I Know
AFK	Away From Keyboard
B4N	Bye For Now
BAK	Back At Keyboard
BBL	Be Back Later
BCNU	Be Seeing You
BEG	Big Evil Grin
BFD	Big F***ing Deal
BFN	Bye For Now
BRB	Be Right Back
BTW	By The Way
CU	See You
CUL, CUL8R	See You Later
DIKU	Do I Know You?
EG	Evil Grin
F2F	Face To Face
FUD	Fear, Uncertainty and Doubt
FWIW	For What Its Worth
FYI	For Your Information
G/<G>	Grin
GA	Go Ahead
GAL	Get A Life
GD&R	Grinning, Ducking and Running
GMTA	Great Minds Think Alike
IAC	In Any Case
IANAL	I Am Not A Lawyer
IC	I See
IIRC	If I Recall/Remember Correctly
IMHO	In My Humble/Honest Opinion
IMO	In My Opinion
IOW	In Other Words
IRL	In Real Life
JK	Just Kidding
L8R	Later
LOL	Laughing Out Loud
NRN	No Reply/Response Necessary
OIC	Oh, I See
OTOH	On The Other Hand
PDA	Public Display of Affection
PITA	Pain In the Arse
RL	Real Life
ROFL	Rolling On Floor Laughing
ROTFL	Rolling On The Floor Laughing
RSN	Real Soon Now
RTFM	Read The F***ing Manual
SNAFU	Situation Normal, All F***ed Up
SO	Significant Other

TANSTAAFL	There Ain't No Such Thing As A Free Lunch
TIA	Thanks In Advance
TPTB	The Powers That Be
TTFN	Ta Ta For Now
TTYL	Talk To You Later
TYVM	Thank You Very Much
VBG	Very Big Grin
WB	Welcome Back
WTH	What The Hell
YMMV	Your Mileage May Vary

Active Movie
Microsoft technology used to download audio and video through the Internet as well as view and listen to them. It is a multimedia *ActiveX* control.

Active Server Pages
See ASP

ActiveX
A language developed by Microsoft in response to Java (a *Sun Microsystems* technology) which allows the creation of interactive web pages which look and behave like computer programs instead of static pages. It has come under severe criticism because of its lack of security, and its use is discouraged by many experts, although it also has many followers, as it facilitates the creation of multimedia web pages. ActiveX controls can be used to create interactive effects such as buttons which change their shape and colour, as well as audio effects that are triggered when the cursor is moved over certain objects or when they are selected. In order to function, the browser must support ActiveX. ActiveX controls can be downloaded from the Internet and offer a functionality similar to that of Java *applets*. Another facility for designers and programers is the ability to include passwords, query databases and other functions not supported by HTML.
Thus, there are ActiveX controls and documents. Controls are objects included within the page, such as buttons which change colour when the mouse is moved over them. Documents are objects that can be watched using a viewer; it is possible to navigate within them.
An interesting reference point for technicians and programers is www.activex.org

ad

An abbreviation of the word 'advertisement'. On the Internet, it refers to publicity on web pages, often taking the form of banners of different shapes and sizes which can incorporate animated text and images. The example shows a banner of a very common size, 460x80 pixels.
See BANNER

ad click
See CLICK RATE

ad rotation
The process by which, every time a web page is opened, a different advertisement appears in a consecutive or random order. This allows the messages of advertisers to be varied, so the same ad does not always appear on the same page. This is

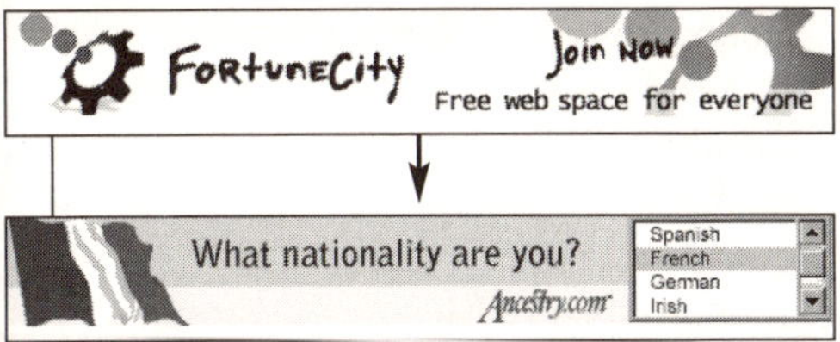

achieved using specific software, usually managed by one of the companies specialising in Internet advertising. For example, an advertisement appears when the 'Home & Family' page of the AltaVista search engine is accessed; if the same web page is accessed a few seconds later, a different advertisement will appear in its place.

ad space
The space within a web page specifically reserved for advertising. Companies which offer ad spaces on the Internet sell them to advertisers in much the same way as slots for television advertisements in commercial breaks.

address
1 e-mail address (See E-MAIL)
2 IP address (See IP ADDRESS)
3 Internet address, also called *URL (Uniform Resource Locator)*. It is the Internet address at which a website or page is located, such as http://www.atkearney/news. When this address is typed into the browser, it connects to and displays that page. The address always begins with 'http://' (*hypertext transfer protocol*), indicating a page on the Web, followed by 'www'. In later versions of some browsers, it is not necessary to type the whole address. The 'www' is a convention and does not always appear. This address is equivalent to a numerical *IP* address.
See URL

address book

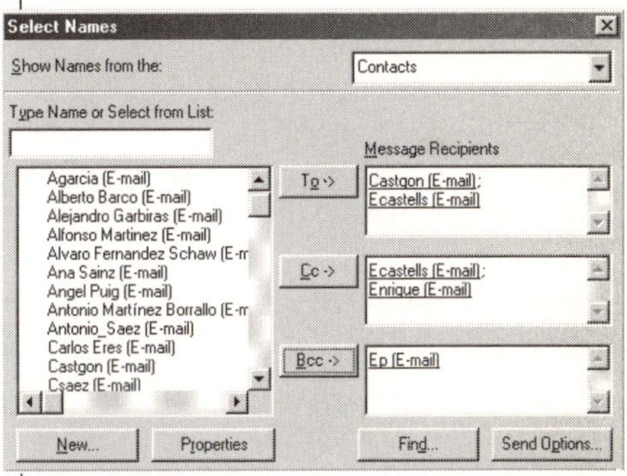

A utility offered by some mail programs that allows users to access their most-used e-mail addresses by name; some browsers also allow the inclusion of additional data, such as nicknames and company names. Address books are a useful and very accessible way of filing e-mail addresses. To add them to a message, they just have to be dragged from the address book to the destination field on the e-mail screen, making it unnecessary to type them out every time or have a physical address book.

address mask
Used to recognise and identify the sections of an *IP* address which are made up of numeric groups separated by full stops. It is also known as 'subnet mask'. For example, a numerical IP Address can be 207.37.253.203, which corresponds to www.atkearney.com.

address sign
See @, AT SIGN

administrator (admin)
From the Latin 'ad' (towards) and 'ministratio' (to serve). It has two distinct meanings:

1 a system administrator (sysadmin), i.e. the individual in charge of a network;
2 the individual in charge of managing and maintaining a mailing list or discussion group on the Internet.

ADSL (Asymmetric Digital Subscriber Line)
A technology which transforms ordinary phone lines (also known as 'twisted copper pairs') into high-speed digital lines which can transmit information at speeds ranging from 1.5 to 9 Mbps downstream and from 16 to 800 Kbps upstream. This is much faster than using regular modems or ISDN, and similar to that of cable modem. The speed is greatly reduced by the distance and quality of the telephone line. XDSL is a generic abbreviation applied to the different types of *DSL (Digital Subscriber Line)* in existence, such as HDSL, RADSL, SDSL or VDSL.

Advanced Research Projects Agency
See ARPA

Advanced Research Projects Agency Network
See ARPANET

affiliate programs
From the Latin 'fidelitas'. In the real world, users of affiliate or loyalty schemes get

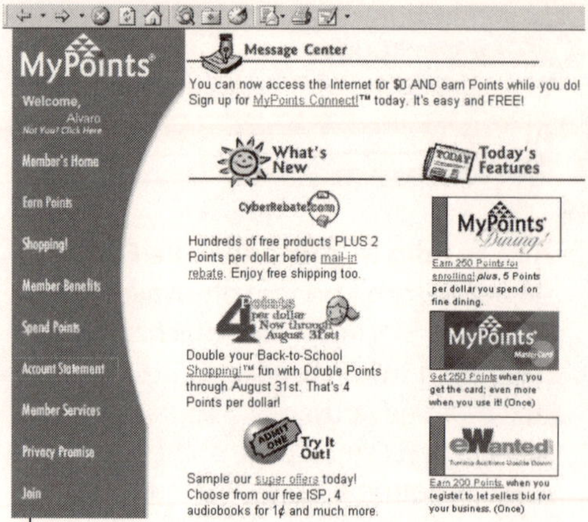

points for travelling with specific airlines, staying in specific hotels, leasing cars, using specific petrol stations, shopping in specific supermarkets, etc. The points can then be redeemed for products and services in the same companies or in others. On the Internet, a number of affiliate programs have appeared, which allow users to get points by surfing through specific websites, answering surveys, buying from e-shops, giving feedback, registering on websites, participating in games and much more. These points can be redeemed at various websites. The following are examples of loyalty websites: www.mypoints. com, www.webmiles.de, www.zakis.com. The screen dump shows one of the pages of mypoints.

agent
An automatic process which carries out a task or series of tasks with little or no human intervention, for example, a filter in an e-mail program which eliminates unauthorised messages. An agent can locate information, complete transactions

and communicate with other users or agents.

AI
See ARTIFICIAL INTELLIGENCE

AIFF (Audio Interchange File Format)
An audio format originally available for the Apple Macintosh but which has since been used by other systems.

alias
An alternate name, nickname or pseudonym which is substituted for the real name, usually because it is short and easy to remember. It can denote a person or group of persons in a network. It is also a system used by e-mail users to replace the complete e-mail address of an individual. Aliases are also used in *IRC* and *chat rooms*, where a short name is used to substitute for a real one in order to hide the individual's identity. For example, in webmaster@atkearney.com, 'Webmaster' is an alias (or nickname) which has been substituted for the real name of the person in charge of receiving e-mail messages. In this case, it indicates the responsibility of the individual for the website. In electronic.business@atkearney.com, the alias belongs to a group of people who are part of an interest or work environment. When an e-mail message is sent to this address, it is automatically sent to all the people on the mailing list.

alignment
Indicates the position of text on a web page. It can be centred, left aligned or right aligned.

alpha
Used for software or hardware in its initial development stages, when it is being tested internally. Alpha programs are not stable and may not include full functionality. After tests and adjustments, the product enters the *beta* stage, which is usually carried out externally with interested companies who collaborate in the testing. For example, before Windows 95 and 98 were launched, many companies and individuals used a beta version to uncover errors and suggest improvements to the product.

.alt (alternate newsgroup)
A major subject category for the alternate *USENET newsgroups*. These non-moderated newsgroups are not official and can be started by anyone who has the time, equipment and knowledge. They enjoy a large number of users and are established hierarchically. The 'alt' hierarchy covers the widest variety of topics, from technical to political or religious, which can be read by its users and where messages can be exchanged.
The alt. category is one of the best known. Others are .comp (computer), .news, .sci (science), .talk, .biz (business), .misc (miscellaneous), .rec (recreational) and .soc (social).
These newsgroups can be accessed through most Internet browsers.
See NEWSGROUPS

AltaVista
A company based in Palo Alto (California) with controlling interest owned by CMGI Inc. The name comes from a blackboard

in a laboratory where some words were partially erased. The word 'Alto' (of Palo Alto) ended up next to the word 'Vista', and someone said, 'How about AltaVista?' Founded in 1995 in the DEC research laboratories, it became property of Compaq Computer Corporation in January 1999. However, at the end of that year, it was sold to CMGI.

It is best known for owning one of the major Internet portals. Its outstanding use is as a search engine, since it has over 100 million indexed pages, as well as *USENET* newsgroups articles.

altavista:

AltaVista's search *robot*, called Scooter, and the indexing system, Ni2, are probably the most powerful and robust available on the Internet. AltaVista indexes all words included in a web page, while other search engines only index key words. This allows searches to achieve a larger number of responses or hits. Its website is www.altavista.com.

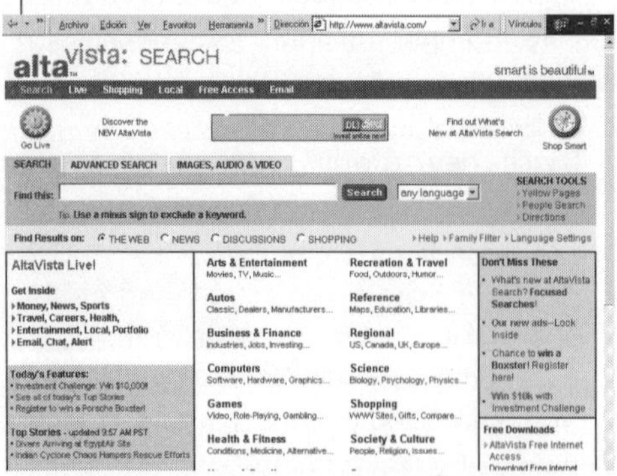

Amazon

amazon.com.

From the Greek 'a' (deprived of) and 'mazos' (breast), referring to the legendary women warriors who supposedly cut off their right breasts in order to use their bows more easily. Amazon is an Internet bookshop created by Jeff Bezos and opened in July 1995. It is one of the pioneering companies in the sale of books over the Internet and currently the undisputed leader in this market, with outlets in several countries such as Germany (www. amazon.de) and the UK (www.amazon.co.uk). It was floated on the stock market in May 1997, with spectacular growth.

By mid-2000, it had more than 20 million customers from 160 countries and has now diversified into toys, videos, music, electronic goods, auctions and other products. Its website is www.amazon.com.

America Online
See AOL

American National Standards Institute
See ANSI

American Registry for Internet Numbers
See ARIN

American Standard Code for Information Interchange
See ASCII

analogue-to-digital (ADC)
The translation of analogue data into a digital format, such as when the content of a video cassette is saved as an Internet video format, such as .mov.

anchor
In HTML, anchors indicate the beginning and end of hypertext links, that is, the departing point and final destination. When users click in the anchor area, they are taken to another area. These areas are usually highlighted in another colour or change colours when the cursor goes over them. It is a synonym of *hyperlink*. In *HTML*, for example, an anchor can be written as <title>AltaVista -Welcome< /title>
See HTML

and, &
A word used as a modifier when conducting Internet searches. It is a *Boolean operator* which, when located between two words, indicates that only documents containing both words must be located. It is usually substituted by the ampersand symbol (&), for example: 'dictionary & spanish'.

angels
See BUSINESS ANGELS

animated GIF
See GIF89a

anonymous FTP (Anonymous File Transfer Protocol)
A service available in thousands of FTP sites on the Internet. It permits anyone to download documents, files and public programs through FTP free of charge and without the need for a user ID or password. In order to access the service, the word 'anonymous' is usually entered as user ID with an e-mail address or another word as the password.

anonymous FTP Site
An FTP site which does not require a user ID and password to be accessed.

ANSI (American National Standards Institute)

Private, non-profit/making organisation founded in 1981 by five engineering associations and three US government agencies. It is currently supported by various public and private organisations and it defends the interests of almost 1,000 companies, organisations, government agencies and national and international institutional members.
ANSI has offices in New York and in Washington D.C. and is responsible for establishing, managing and co-ordinating technical standards within the US, sometimes differing from those established by the *IOS*, but it is not responsible for the development of the ANS (American National Standards). ANSI participates in the definition of standard network protocols.

It represents the United States in the IOS (International Organisation for Standardisation), of which it is a founder member, and in the IEC (International Electrotechnical Commission). Its website is www.ansi.org.

antispam technologies
Technologies, usually software based, which prevent the reception of unsolicited e-mail (known as *spam*).
See SPAM

antivirus software/program

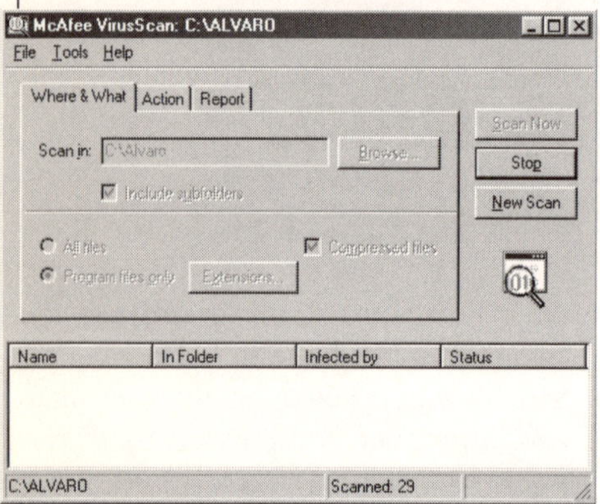

A program that stops viruses gaining access to computers, or finds and eliminates them once they have gained access.

antivirus scanner
An application which checks the system in order to identify possible viruses and eliminate them or prevent them gaining access. It is possible to get viruses through FTP, files sent as e-mail attachments or by downloading applications and files from web pages.

AOL (America Online)

A company founded in Virginia in 1985 which provides Internet access to more than 23 million users plus an additional 2.8 million users acquired through the purchase of *CompuServe*, which was the company's main competitor in the US. In late 1998, it purchased Netscape jointly with *Sun* for four billion dollars.
Its service is used as a portal to the Internet by an ever-growing number of new users, since it offers a high level of functionality at low cost. It is common to see e-mail users with AOL addresses, i.e. name@aol.com.

AOLer
Name given to AOL users.

Apache

The Apache Software Foundation
http://www.apache.org/

A powerful and very flexible HTTP server which includes the latest available protocols. It is very adaptable and can be extended with third-party developed modules. It is a web server, not an application

server, and does not include database functionality; it works with Windows NT and 9x, Netware 5.x, OS/2 and most versions of *UNIX* platforms.
Its name comes from 'A PAtCHy server', since it is based on existing codes and a series of patch files. For some developers, it is also a tribute to the Apache North American Indian tribe of the Atabasco group.
As opposed to Internet server software programs for which a licence fee has to be paid, Apache offers a quality product used by over half of existing Internet servers and which is freely distributed.
Lately, Netscape and Microsoft software has gained strength and is reducing Apache's market share. By February 2000, there were six million servers worldwide using Apache.
There is no official technical support for Apache. Problem-solving support can be found through several *USENET* newsgroups and companies which offer it commercially. Its website is www.apache.org.

API (Application Programming Interface)
An interface that allows two incompatible pieces of software to communicate with each other. Documentation for programers includes the technical specifications needed to create the interfaces.
On the Internet, APIs permit the extension of web-server capabilities. Some well-known server APIs are:
ISAPI: Microsoft Internet Information Server;
NSAPI: Netscape Commerce and Enterprise Server;
WSAPI: O'Reilly Web Site and Web Site Pro.

application
Software designed to perform specific tasks for the user, and defined by that same user. On the Internet, well-known applications are FTP, e-mail client, Gopher, browsers and Telnet.

APNIC (Asia Pacific Network Information Centre)

A non-profit-making organisation responsible for managing and registering *IP (Internet Protocol)* addresses in the Asia-Pacific region, including Japan, Korea, China and Australia. It is one of three worldwide 'Regional Internet Registries' which jointly supply registration services throughout the world.
See ARIN and RIPE NCC. Its website is www.apnic.net.

AppleLink
Apple BBS (Bulletin Board System/Service) for users of their Macintosh computers.
See BBS

applet
Diminutive of 'application'. An applet is a small application or program, written in the object-oriented *Java* programing language which can only function within another program. It allows a web page to include special audio and video effects, interactive animations, changes in graphics

or colours, or to perform specific computing or data-exchange tasks, such as instantaneous calculations and other simple functions that do not require a request from the user to the server which hosts the page.
Java applets remain embedded in the *HTML* page and are sent to the user along with it; they differ from pure Java applications in that they cannot access some resources in the local computer, such as files or peripherals (printers, modem), and they cannot read or write data in the client computer, that is, they have a very strict security control and restrictions which prevent their harming the user's computer or downloading a virus.
They can only read and write data which come from the domain which supplied them. Java applets require the use of a Java-enabled browser. When the web page with the Java applet is accessed, the browser downloads it from the server and makes it perform in the user's computer. In order to use an applet within a page, the applet's name must be specified, as well as its size (length and height) in pixels.
Before the Web existed, drawing or word-processing programs included in Windows were also sometimes called applets.

Application Programing Interface
See API

Archie (ARCHIve sErver)
Used to denote the search tool for *anonymous FTP* sites. Archie (the name comes from its similarity to the word 'archive') was developed by the McGill School of Computer Science, but is no longer used to conduct searches through the files of the thousands of FTP servers which offer anonymous access, having been replaced by the more powerful search engines on the Internet. Currently, it is used to visit every anonymous FTP site, read all the names of directories and files and then catalogue and index them; Archie has an index of over 1,200 FTP sites. When searches are conducted, this large index compares the query with its data and locates the required files and software. When a search with a file name is conducted, Archie returns a list of all the places where it can be found. Search queries can be made through e-mail, Gopher or web search engines.
Archie is very similar to *Veronica*, which indexes *gopher* servers.
See ANONYMOUS FTP

archive
1 Place where software, data and other materials are stored. *FTP* sites are known as archives.
2 To place several documents in a single file in order to facilitate tasks such as back-up, management and transmission. Program archives are usually compressed for easy transmission or storage.

archive site
Server which provides users of the Internet an organised way to access files.

ARIN (American Registry for Internet Numbers)
Non-profit-making organisation created for the management and registration of

ARIN

IP (Internet Protocol) addresses in the geographical areas of North and South America, the Caribbean and sub-Saharan Africa. It was formed December 1997 with authorisation from the NSF (National Science Foundation) and, by agreement with the *IANA*, has taken over from *InterNIC* the management of *IP numbers*. It is one of the three worldwide Regional Internet Registries which jointly give registration services throughout the world. It can be visited at www.arin.net

.arj
Archive program created by Robert Jung which permits the compression of documents on MS-DOS and other operating systems.

ARPA (Advanced Research Projects Agency)
Also known as *ARPANet*, this is a US Defence Department Agency whose creation directive was signed in February 1958. It is known for promoting the development of the Internet until early 1969.
In March 1972, its name was changed to *DARPA (Defence Advanced Research Projects Agency)* and it was established as a separate defence agency.
In February 1993, it went back to being called ARPA, under President Clinton's administration, and in February 1996, it changed back again to DARPA.
See DARPA and ARPANet.

ARPANet (Advanced Research Projects Agency Network)
The forerunner of the Internet, developed in the late sixties (1969) and early seventies by the US Defence Department. It was a cold-war experiment to achieve a wide-area computer network (*WAN*) that could survive an eventual nuclear war with the USSR. It was designed in such a way that there was no central computer; instead, it had many computers over a wide geographical area. Thus, if even a large part of the network were destroyed, the rest would continue operating. This was made possible by transmitting information through the network in packets, so if one of the connections was broken, packets would automatically be re-routed. After military use, the main application of the network was that of research and development, universities, education centres and, finally, all commercial and social sectors.
Developed by Bolt, Beranek and Newman, the first ARPANet connection was established in November 1969 between the University of California at Los Angeles (UCLA) and the Stanford Research Institute (SRI). For a time, ARPANet was divided into Milnet and a new ARPANet. Milnet connected military sites, while the new ARPANet connected other sites, mainly from universities. Thus, in the eighties, ARPANet was replaced by a new, separate military network, the *Defence Data Network (DDN)*, and the *NSFNet*, a network of scientific and academic computers founded by the NSF (National Science Foundation). A new communications protocol, *TCP/IP*, was developed to allow for

the large number of interconnections carried out on the network.
In 1995, NSFNet became the *backbone* of the Internet as it exists today, along with a consortium of backbone providers such as Sprint, MCI, PSINet, UUNET, ANS/AOL and AGIS-Net99.
ARPANet has since been dismantled.

ARPU (Average Revenue Per User)
The average income that an Internet business obtains per user per year (or, occasionally, month). It is used, for example, by *ISPs (Internet Service Providers)* to measure the average income they get from their subscribers.

articles
Name given to messages placed for reading in *newsgroups*.

artificial intelligence
Area of computing which works on the simulation of human intelligence in computer systems.

AS
See AUTONOMOUS SYSTEM

ASCII (American Standard Code for Information Interchange)
ASCII files are those which use the 128 alphanumeric and special control characters which can be coded with seven binary digits (seven-bit code). The 128 ASCII standard codes represent seven-digit numbers ranging from 0000000 to 1111111. Some Internet protocols, such as simple mails and newsgroups, can only support eight-bit code.
The extended ASCII character set also contains 128 decimal numbers ranging from 128 to 255, which represent special graphic, mathematical and foreign characters. Word-processing files which include special characters are coded in eight binary digits. ASCII code allows a number to be assigned to each key on the computer's keyboard. Out of the 256 characters, the first 128 are standard, of which the first 32 are control codes and the following 96 are standard characters representing numbers, letters of the Roman alphabet (upper and lower case), as well as punctuation marks and special characters. The last 128 characters represent different things in different platforms.
ASCII format is one of the most commonly found, since it is used for basic text files which do not contain formatting information and do not need special programs in order to be accessed, so they can be read by most computers. They are also known as plain-text files or ASCII files.

ASCII file
See ASCII

ASCII text file
See ASCII

Asia Pacific Network Information Centre
See APNIC

Ask Jeeves
An interesting search engine which allows queries to be couched in the same terms as if speaking to a human being. For example, in order to search for a ho-

tel in London, the query to a standard search engines would be 'hotels & London'; in Ask Jeeves, it would be 'I want information about modern hotels in the city of London', i.e. the question is posed in natural-sounding language. The answer would be in the form of a list of hotels in the city. The system learns from the users' questions, so as to be increasingly effective.
Ask Jeeves was created in 1996 in California by Garrett Gruener and David Warthen. In 1997, its first website was launched, www.askjeeves.com, which was followed in 1998 by www.ajkids.com, targeted at children.
Its website is www.ask.com.

ASP (Active Server Pages)
Technology developed by Microsoft which permits the combination of *HTML*, *JavaScript*, Microsoft VBScript and *ActiveX* components in an open environment from its proprietary web-server software (Microsoft Internet Information Server), creating very powerful web-based solutions.
When a browser requests an ASP page, the web server generates a tailored HTML page and delivers it to the browser. Pages thus created use the '.asp' extension.
ASP is more dependable than *CGI* scripts, where a large number of client requests must be managed.

ASP (Application Service Provider)
ASPs are companies, in many instances providing telecommunication services, which offer the use of application software to other companies, hosting it in their own servers and facilities, so their clients do not have to purchase the software, paying only for its use and accessing the applications through the Internet. For example, a company can remotely use an accounting program hosted on an ASP.

Asynchronous Transfer Mode
See ATM

at
See @

at sign
See @

ATM (Asynchronous Transfer Mode)
Communication between two computers in which signals are sent in irregular or asynchronous intervals. Each character is preceded by a start bit and followed by a stop bit.
This kind of transmission allows a character to be sent some time after the previous character without any attention paid to the time lapse. If there is noise in the line, the modem can wait for the appropriate moment to start sending the next byte. Packets are small and of a fixed size, and routing, managing and priority decisions are intelligent. This permits some data, such as video or voice data, to be assembled quickly and efficiently.
It is also called 'fast packet', since it permits a high transmission speed.

attachment, attached file
One or more files included in an e-mail message. Files can be included in practically any e-mail program. The attached file is translated into ASCII text through *MIME* or *BinHex* and is then sent through the mail system. When the addressee gets the e-mail message with the attached file, his own e-mail software translates it into a file which then recovers its original form. This enables the transmission of all types of file through e-mail. Files can include graphics, audio, video, etc.

.au
Common audio file developed by *Sun Microsystems* for *UNIX* systems. Other well-known formats are MIDI and WAV.

audio/video interleaved
See .AVI

AUP (Acceptable Use Policy)
The formal rules that must be followed when using the Internet so as not to bother other users, e.g.

1 Do not put any illegal or forbidden material, or certain free-access pornographic materials, up on the Internet.
2 Do not use the Internet to break the law.
3 Do not break the security systems of other computers on the Internet.
4 Do not send mass unwanted mail messages (*spam*).
5 Do not start *flaming* wars in the *newsgroups*.
6 Do not send overwhelming quantities of data to servers in order to block them.
7 Do not put up commercial advertisement in forbidden places, such as newsgroups.

In many cases, users not complying with any of these norms are denied access by their *ISP*. Aternatively, judicial action may be taken, as is the case with child pornography.
AUP norms are usually established by ISPs, universities, networks and other organisations which offer Internet services, and must be accepted by the user. Up until 1994, *NSFNet* forbade commercial and non-academic activities on the Internet, but this rule was so continuously broken that it was eliminated, allowing for the development of the present business Internet.
See NETIQUETTE

authentication

Identification of a user in order to allow access to a system or network to make changes. It generally depends on a password, login (user ID), cardkey or other system to check that the user trying to gain access is the authorised person. The example shows the authentication system required to enter and operate in E*Trade. If the password has been forgotten, there is a link to a system for a reminder.

authoring, web authoring
The creation of web pages using *HTML* or other codes. The term ‘authoring’ includes layout and design as well as writing.

auto-response, autoresponder, auto-response mailbox

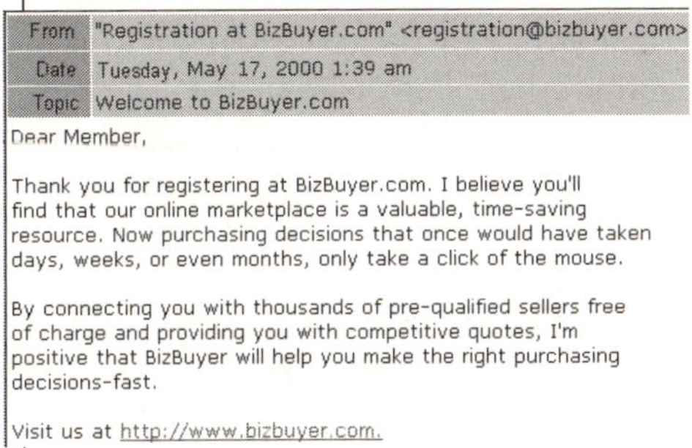

From	"Registration at BizBuyer.com" <registration@bizbuyer.com>
Date	Tuesday, May 17, 2000 1:39 am
Topic	Welcome to BizBuyer.com

Dear Member,

Thank you for registering at BizBuyer.com. I believe you'll find that our online marketplace is a valuable, time-saving resource. Now purchasing decisions that once would have taken days, weeks, or even months, only take a click of the mouse.

By connecting you with thousands of pre-qualified sellers free of charge and providing you with competitive quotes, I'm positive that BizBuyer will help you make the right purchasing decisions-fast.

Visit us at http://www.bizbuyer.com.

An electronic mail system which is set up to automatically respond to e-mail messages, subscription or service requests from a website. These response messages are usually pre-formatted standard replies. For example, an e-mail message requesting a book from a publishing house on the Internet can receive an answer message saying thank you for the purchase and recommending other similar books. This is an automated mailing and is usually sent immediately. The image shows the automated response message for registering at Bizbuyer.

avatar
A hindu word which denotes the reincarnation of a god in human or animal form. Best known because of the legend of the god Vishnu and his ten reincarnations, of which the first nine have already happened, in all of which he brought good upon the land.
On the Internet, it means the graphic representation (icon) of a person in a *chat*, 3D (three-dimensional) or Internet game environment. It is the form adopted when entering a digital world, where a user can appear under the guise of an animal, an object, a cartoon, etc. The avaturs of other users can be seen on the screen, creating the impression of a virtual world.

average revenue per user
See ARPU

.avi, AVI (Audio/Video Interleaved, audio/visual interface)
Format created by Microsoft to allow the digital storage of high-quality video (images and sound). These files can be included in presentations (such as in Microsoft PowerPoint) or web pages. Documents stored in this format have the '.avi' extension and require a compatible reader, usually included in the browser or downloadable from the Internet. Another frequently used format is QuickTime, developed by Apple.

B2B
Business to Business. Relationships between companies via the Internet.

B2C
Business to Consumer. Relationships between companies and consumers via the Internet.

B2E
Business to Employee. Relationships between companies and their workers via the Internet.

back button

A button located on the browser toolbar with enables the user to return to previously visited pages.

backbone
The main international telecommunications network, the 'spinal column' which carries Internet traffic to other national, regional and local networks. It is also a high-speed line or a series of connections which make up a major trajectory within a network.
The backbone is so-called because of its similarity with the spinal cord and its ancillary nervous system. On the Internet, it is the core of all connections and transfers made, and it is the highest level in a hierarchical network. All other networks connect to the backbone. They are usual ly fibre-optic lines with a very high capacity and speed.
The original network established by the US National Science Foundation (NSF) today has multiple backbones belonging to telecommunications suppliers such as MCI, Sprint, UUNET or AT&T.
Usually, *ISPs* which offer Internet access to the public themselves pay a fee for access to the backbone and then re-sell the service to the consumer.

background
The colour, graphic or image used behind the text and main images on a web page.

bandwidth
1 A measure of the quantity of information which can be transmitted over a specific time on a network (such as the Internet) or a telephone line. The usual measure is *bits per second (bps)*, although *Kilobits per second (Kbps)* or *Megabits per second (Mbps)* are also used. A larger bandwidth means a larger amount of data (information) can travel at the same time. New technologies, such as ISDN and cable modem, afford the user a larger bandwidth.
A page of text holds around 15,000 bits. A quick modem can transfer over 30,000 bits per second. When creating web pages, it is important to take into account the size of images and graphics included in it, so it does not demand excessive bandwidth for its trans-

mission and make the page slow to download. Video sequences take up the most bandwidth. Previously, when Internet content was essentially text, acceptable information download times could be achieved with a slow modem. Today, pages use abundant images, graphics and animations, which makes for slower download.

Alternatively, when several users access the Internet simultaneously, they share bandwidth, which can also make for slow downloads, and speed will not improve even if a faster modem is used.

Most people surfing the Internet use dial-up modems, generally with a speed of 14.4, 28.8 or, more frequently, 56 Kbps.

2 In analogue terms (as opposed to digital), the frequency transmission width (range) of a channel measured in cycles per second or hertz, kilohertz, megahertz, etc.

3 Hacker jargon: if someone says they are 'high bandwidth', they mean they can process high amounts of information in short periods of time.

banner

Commercial ads on the Internet. They are usually rectangular or, less-commonly, square, and they almost always have movement in the form of sequential images which repeat themselves endlessly (animated *GIFs*); the animation attracts more visitors than static images. Rectangular banners can have different sizes; among the most common are 460x60 and 120x90 pixels.

As with other commercial advertisements, they are usually paid for, but sometimes they are included free of charge, as part of a banner exchange between two websites. They can usually be found in commercial or sponsored websites.

The visitor to the host page can click on the banners (where there are links) and access the advertised website or offer.

Rectangular banners can usually be found on the top or bottom of the pages and square banners on the sides.

Advertising impact is measured as 'banner views', i.e. the number of banners seen of that ad in that website. A more precise measurement is the number of

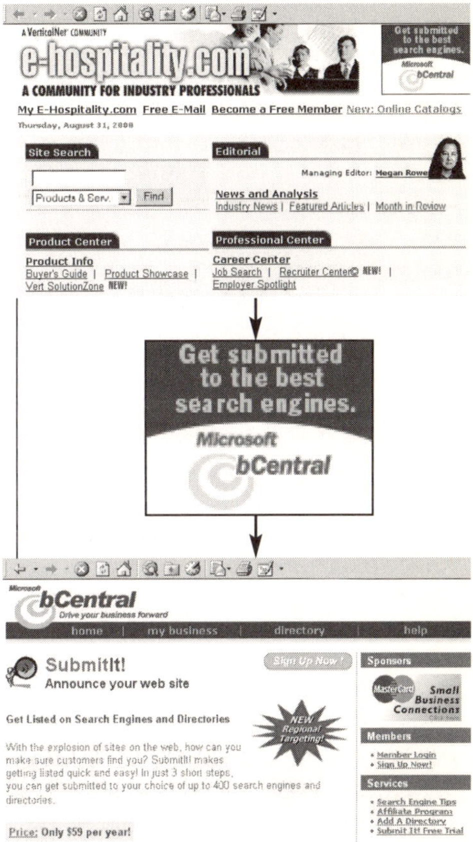

users who click on the banner and visit the main advertisement site.
The example shows the site of the vertical portal www.e-hospitality.com, with a 120x90 pixel banner on the top, to the right. Clicking on the banner will takes us to www.sitemanager.bcentralcom.

baud
From Jean Maurice Emile Baudot, a French engineer who died in 1903 and who was the first to use the word for measuring the transmission speed of telegraph signals. A baud equals one change of electronic state per second.
It is the usual measurement to determine the speed of *modems* and other devices capable of transmitting data, which is technically determined by the number of events or signal changes per second.
Generally, the baud rate shows the number of *bits* that a modem can transmit or receive per second. Although it is technically incorrect, baud and *bits per second* have been used interchangeably. Baud rate is usually — and equivocally — confused with the number of bits per second (bps).
Formerly, when 300-baud modems were used, each signal represented one bit of information (the signal could only have two states), so the baud rate and the transfer velocity of a modem (expressed in bits per second, bps) were the same: 300 baud was 300 bits per second. However, this changes in higher-speed modems. A modem with a speed of 1,200 bits per second works at 300 baud, but moves four bits per baud (four bits times 300 baud = 1,200 bits per second). A 28,800 modem works at 2,400 baud, but each signal carries 12 bits of information, so the data-transfer speed is 28,800 bits per second. Modems are available with the following baud rates: 2,400, 9,600, 14,400, 28,800, 33,600 and 56,000 bps; however, 2,400 and 9,600 modems are now almost obsolete, and the most commonly used modem at present is 56,000. They are also expressed in Kilobits per second, for example, 28.8 Kbps. ISDN lines allow 64 or 128 Kbps, and T1 lines 1.45 Megabits per second.

baud rate
A measure of data-transfer speed used, among others, to determine the speed of a *modem*.
See BAUD

BBBOnLine (Better Business Bureau On Line)

An offshoot of the Better Business Bureau, created in 1997 with the aim of promoting privacy on the Internet. Internet compa-

nies which belong to its 'BBBOnLine Reliability' program must be active for at least a year and accept BBB's advertising standards and dispute resolution systems.
The presence of the BBBOnLine seal guarantees that a website follows the established norms.
For the child sector, there is the 'BBBOnLine Kid's Privacy' seal, which guarantees that the company displaying it agrees with the ethical principles related to children's privacy. The previons page shows the three logos which appear on pages affiliated to the system. Its website is at www.bbbonline.org

BBS (Bulletin Board System/Service)
Private computer service (usually a single Mac or PC computer) which became widespread in the 1970s, which users can access through dial-up connection or through the Internet. It allows users to place and receive e-mail messages, access mailing lists, discussion groups, databases and files or even make shared purchases. They usually cover particular areas of interest or specific geographical zones. They are usually created and maintained by individual non-professionals, although many are the property of educational, government or research institutions. Until a few years ago, there were over 50,000 worldwide, covering subjects such as leisure, education, legislation or games. There are free BBSs, but most charge for access through subscription and are usually accessed by users in the same area, since telephone calls are local, and users in other areas would incur excessive costs when accessing remote BBSs. Most BBSs have ended up being part of the Internet and even offer an access service to it, making it likely that, before too long, they will all become part of the Internet. These BBSs can also be accessed by Telnet, thus eliminating the cost of long-distance telephone calls for users connecting from outside the area in which the service is located.
BBSs offer group communication similar to those of *LISTSERV* and *USENET* News.

bcc:, to bcc: (blind carbon copy)

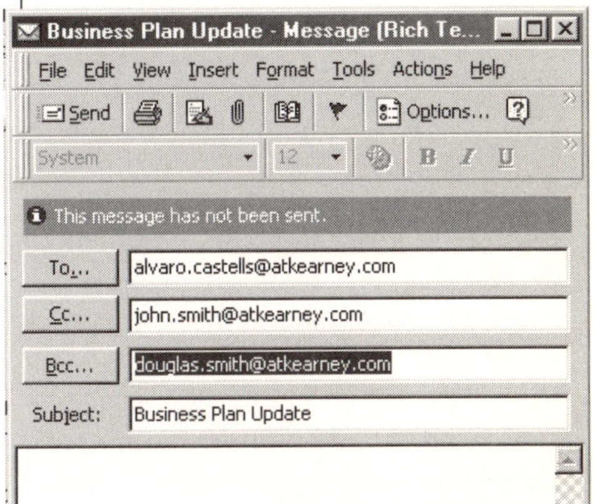

A copy of an e-mail message which is sent to another person or persons without the knowledge of the addressee.
See CC:

bean
See JAVABEANS

Berkeley Internet Name Domain
See BIND

Berners-Lee, Tim
British Oxford graduate who, in 1989, invented the *World Wide Web* while work-

ing at *CERN*. In 1990, he established the first web client and server, using mostly communications software, and defined *URL*, *HTTP* and *HTML*. He later developed his career at *MIT (Massachusetts Institute of Technology)* and chaired the World Wide Web Consortium, an open forum of companies and organisations aiming to develop the Web in order to achieve its full potential.
He was elected one of the 100 personalities of the century by Time Magazine.

beta, beta test
An indication that a computer program is not yet tested enough in order to be commercialised (i.e. it is likely there are still some *bugs* to be eliminated). A program is usually described as being 'under beta', 'beta test' or 'in beta testing'. The beta version of a software program is usually tested both in the manufacturing company as well as by collaborating developers and computer integrators (beta testers), or even end users, in order to subsequently progress to its final launch. Besides software tests, the term can also be used for hardware, websites or services.
The beta test is conducted after the alpha test (alpha and beta being the first two letters of the Greek alphabet). Usually, the alpha test includes testing the system and its components within the company, and the beta test is the one prior to the commercial launch, so it is performed outside the company.
See ALPHA

Bible
In computer terms, the book which contains all the existing knowledge on a specific subject, such as an operating system, program or platform. For example, 'The Macintosh Bible', 'The Internet Bible', etc.

binary
Numerical system made up of zeros and ones, combined in order to represent computer data. All computer systems use binary codes made up of eight, 16 or 32 digits. All the characters on a keyboard are formed by eight binary digits, for example the code 01000001 represents the letter A and 00000010 represents the number two.
See ASCII, BIT

binary code
See BINARY

binary digit
See BIT

binary files
Non-*ASCII* files, usually programs, video or sound. They include up to 256 different characters, combining eight binary digits (*bits*) for each character. ASCII files only use 128 different characters.

BIND (Berkeley Internet Name Domain)
An implementation of *DNS (Domain Name System)* protocols which allows for distributed database capability in such a way that many DNS servers work jointly in order to translate Internet domain names into *IP addresses*. It was developed by the University of California at Berkeley.
See DNS

BinHex (BINary HEXadecimal)
A system to convert non-ASCII files (usually coming from an Apple Macintosh) into ASCII so they can be sent by e-mail.
See MIME, UUENCODE

bit
An abbreviation of 'binary digit', it is the smallest data unit that a computer handles, represented by zero or one (indicating 'off' and 'on' respectively). Eight bits form a *byte*. Lower-case 'b' is used in abbreviations to indicate bits (a capital 'B' refers to bytes). For example, *Kbps* is a thousand bits per second, and this figure, multiplied by eight, equals KBps, or a thousand bytes per second.
A 28.8-Kbps modem can transmit 28.8 thousand bits (Kilobits) per second; thus, its transmission capacity is measured in bits per second, while storage is measured in bytes.

Bit measurements
1 Kb (Kilobit) = 1,024 bits
1 Kbps (Kilobit per second) = 1,000 bits per second
1 Mb (Megabit) = 1,000 Kb or 1,048,576 bits
1 Mbps (Megabit per second) = 1 Megabit per second or 1,000,000 bits per second

Byte measurements
1 KB (Kilobyte) = 1,000 bytes
1 KBps (Kilobyte per second) = 1,000 bytes per second
1 MB (Megabyte) = 1,000 Kilobytes
1 MBps (Megabyte per second)
1 GB (Gigabyte) = 1000 Megabytes
1 GBps (Gigabyte per second)
1 TB (Terabyte) = 1,000 Gigabytes
1 TBps (Terabyte per second)
1 PB (Petabyte) = 1,000 Terabytes
1 PBps (Petabyte per second)
See BYTE

bitmap file
Image format defined by screen dots or pixels. It is represented as '.bmp'.

BITNET (Because It's Time NETwork/ Because It's There NETwork)
An outdated international computer network with several thousand main computers devoted to research and education. It was used for e-mail, mailing lists and file transfer.
This network was separate from the Internet, but e-mails could be exchanged between both networks through bridges that joined BITNET with the Internet.
BITNET was managed by EDUCOM and was split into three major geographic areas: BITNET in the United States and Mexico, NETNORTH in Canada and EARN in Europe. There are also connections in Asia and South America.
LISTSERVs, discussion groups through e-mail, originated in BITNET.

The network was made up of IBM mainframes using the RSCS protocol and a VMS operating system. It did not use *TCP/IP* protocols and has been put aside by the Internet.
See CERN

bits per second
See BPS

.biz (biz newsgroup)
Highest-level *USENET* newsgroup hierarchy devoted to business topics.
Other newsgroups categories are .alt (alternative), .news, .comp (computer), .sci (science), .talk, .misc (miscellaneous), .rec (recreational) and .soc (social).
These newsgroups can be accessed through most Internet browsers.
See NEWSGROUPS

Blade Runner

A movie well beyond its time, filmed in 1982 by Ridley Scott, starring Harrison Ford, Rutger Hauer, Sean Young and Daryl Hanna. Rick Deckhard stalks a steel and technology jungle in Los Angeles, 2019. He is a 'blade runner' hunting a group of rebel replicants who strive to be human. Along with *Matrix*, it is a cult movie in the Internet community.

blind carbon copy
See BCC:

blue ribbon

BLUE RIBBON CAMPAIGN

The *EFF* and other groups who defend freedom of expression in the Internet have extended this symbol throughout many websites which, by displaying it, show their support for the basic human right of freedom of expression.

BOL

bol.com™

Bertelsmann Online, a company belonging to the Bertelsmann group devoted to the sale of books, music, gifts and other products on the Internet.
Along with Amazon and Barnes & Noble, it is one of the top three Internet booksellers.It started operating in Germany and France, and later opened websites in the UK, the Netherlands, Spain and

Switzerland. By mid-2000, it was present in 14 countries and offered more than five million book titles and 800,000 different CDs. Its website is at www.bol.com

bookmark, favourite, hotlist

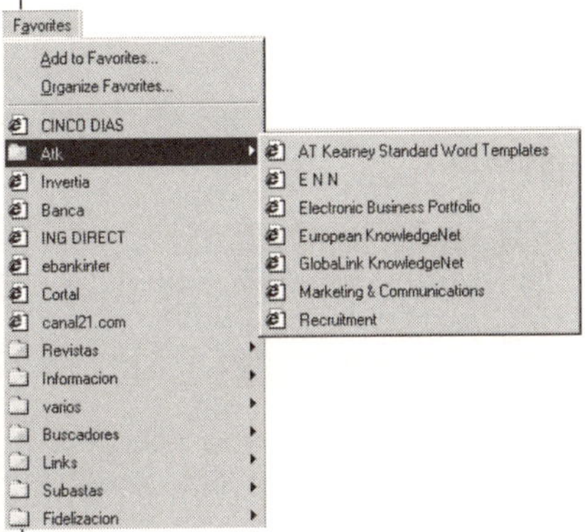

Used in a browser, in much the same way as a traditional, tangible bookmark, to tag an Internet page or website of particular interest. Pages can be tagged as a bookmark or favourite via a pull-down menu in the browser. Tagged pages can be accessed directly just by selecting from its address the pull-down list.
Bookmarks can be arranged in folders, which is extremely useful when there are a large number of them. The bookmark list is called the 'booklist' or 'hotlist'. A useful piece of advice is to rename them before or after storing them, as their names are sometimes too long or can be hard to recognise.
The best-known browsers include a preset list of favourites with which they usually have business agreements, which are companies belonging to the browser manufacturer or which are useful addresses for surfing the net.
Microsoft generally calls them favourites, *Netscape* calls them bookmarks and *Mosaic* and *Opera* call them hotlists. In Microsoft and Netscape, in order to add a bookmark, simply go to the top of the browser window and in the 'Favourites' or 'Bookmark' menu select 'Add to favourites' or 'Add bookmark'; a window may open with the name of the page (which can be changed) and by clicking 'Accept', it will be included in the folder.
To access them, just use the pull-down menu or click on the corresponding browser icon.

bookmark list
See BOOKMARK

bookmarking

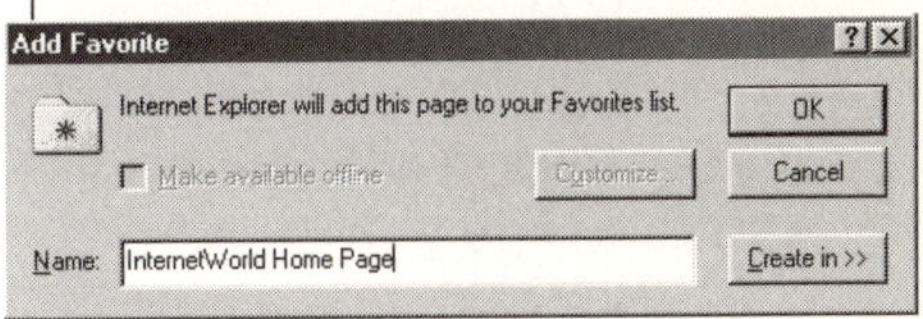

The action of storing frequently-used web addresses in the *bookmark* or favourites folder.
See BOOKMARK

Boolean, Boolean operators
Words or symbols that permit users to conduct more precise searches. The most common Boolean operators are 'and', 'or' and 'not', which allow the search to be restricted or broadened.

In searches, 'and' is used between two words to indicate that documents must contain both words, not just one of them. 'Or' is used to locate documents that contain at least one of the two words. For example, to find information on bookstores in Spain, place the word 'and' between 'bookstores' and 'Spain' to restrict the search to websites and pages which include both concepts.
Boolean search algorithms are based on the algebraic theories of the British mathematician George Boole (1815–1864), who specialised in logical and mathematical problems.

Boolean logic
See BOOLEAN

Boolean search
See BOOLEAN

bot
An abbreviation of 'robot'.
See SPIDER

bottleneck
A restriction in a system's capacity which can reduce traffic when overloaded.

bounce, bounce message, bounced mail
The returning, or 'bouncing', of an e-mail message which has been rejected for some reason, for example:
· The user name or the domain were incorrectly typed.
· The addressee does not exist.
· The message includes a large document which exceeds the quota assigned to the addressee's mailbox. This happens frequently with users who have mailboxes limited to five or ten Megabytes, such as those of free web e-mail accounts.
· A failure in the network or the server.
The message is returned with the 'Undeliverable mail' or 'Message Undeliverable' indication. This is automatically generated by the *Postmaster*.

bps (bits per second)
A measure used to indicate data-transmission speed in *modems* and carriers. Speed in bps equals the number of bits sent or received every second. Larger measures are used to refer to data transmission at higher speeds, such as *Kilobits per second* or kbps, which equals 1,000 bps, or *Megabits per second* (Mbps) equalling 1,000,000 bps.
Earlier modems sent 300, 600, 1,200, 2,400, 9,600, 14,400 and 28,800 bps. Most modern modems transmit 33.6 and 56 Kbps over conventional telephone lines. ISDN lines offer speeds of 128 Kbps, and cable modems usually operate at 256 or 512 Kbps. Computers with *Ethernet* connections operate at 56 Kbps or 1 Mb, and the Internet backbone at 45 Mb.
Another measure related to this is 'number of characters transmitted per second', or cps, which is obtained by dividing the bps rate by ten. Thus, for example, a 14,400 bps modem transmits 1,440 cps.

broadband
A high-speed and capacity transmission channel which allows the simultaneous transmission of video, voice and data. Transmission is carried out through coax-

ial or fibre-optic cables which allow for a larger bandwidth than conventional telephone lines.
See @HOME, @WORK

browser, web browser
A program which uses *HTTP protocol* to allow users to *surf* through the Internet's websites. Browsers enable the use of *e-mail*, *Telnet*, *FTP*, *USENET* newsgroups or *Gopher*. The best known are *Netscape* Communicator (formerly Netscape Navigator) and *Microsoft* Internet Explorer. Others with a smaller market share are *Opera*, *Mosaic* (which appeared in 1992 and was the first graphic browser to be used), *Cello* and the text-based *Lynx*.

browser war
Phrase popularised by the commercial battle between *Netscape* and *Microsoft* for control of the Internet *browser* market. Advertising campaigns, price-slashing up to the point of offering the product for free, law suits, continuous launching of upgraded versions, etc. were used in this war.

bug
A programing error which causes a malfunction when certain aspects of the software are used. Bugs can range from minimal errors that hardly affect the program to failures that crash it or generate errors in the operating system.
The name derives from the damage that can be caused by an insect in computer circuits.

bulletin board
See BBS

Business 2.0

Magazine launched in August 1998 which has become one of the favourites of people interested in the Internet environment. It includes numerous articles relating to business and its evolution. Its website is at www.business2.com

business angels, angels
Rich people who invest in others' start-up businesses, generally giving them the economic boost they need to get off the ground. As this phrase is not exclusive to the Internet, it should perhaps be 'e-business angels' instead.

business to business
See B2B

business to consumer
See B2C

business to employee
See B2E

byte
A measurement unit for data storage. A byte is made up of eight bits and represents one character. The combinations of zeros and ones represent numbers from

zero to 255. Thus, 10100110 is one byte of information. Each byte stores only one information character, which can be a letter, number or symbol (e.g. $, ?, …). Bytes are represented by a capital 'B' in order to distinguish them from bits (b); therefore *KBps* represents a thousand bytes per second. A 28.8 Kbps *modem* can transmit 28.8 thousand bits (Kilobits) per second, so the transmission capability is measured in bits per second, while storage is measured in bytes.

Bit measurements

1 Kb (Kilobit) = 1,024 bits
1 Kbps (Kilobit per second) = 1,000 bits per second
1 Mb (Megabit) = 1,000 Kb or 1,048,576 bits
1 Mbps (Megabit per second) = 1 Megabit per second or 1,000,000 bits per second

Byte measurements

1 KB (Kilobyte) = 1,000 bytes
1 KBps (Kilobyte per second) = 1,000 bytes per second
1 MB (Megabyte) = 1,000 Kilobytes
1 MBps (Megabyte per second)
1 GB (Gigabyte) = 1000 Megabytes
1 GBps (Gigabyte per second)
1 TB (Terabyte) = 1,000 Gigabytes
1 TBps (Terabyte per second)
1 PB (Petabyte) = 1,000 Terabytes
1 PBps (Petabyte per second)
See BIT

C
Programing language developed in the 1970s to create professional applications.

C++
Programing language based on C language that includes object-oriented design.

C2C (Consumer to Consumer)
In general, commercial relations between individual consumers on the Internet such as second-hand dealing between individuals.

Cable TV, CATV (Community Antenna Television)
A television delivery system that, in contrast to satellite and terrestrial television, connects the user via a cable. Cable television offers the possibility of connecting to the Internet, using e-mail, etc.

cache
In the Internet environment, the cache memory is a storage area in the computer in which most common browsers (Microsoft and Netscape) store recently visited pages, with their text, sound, *URLs*, graphics and images. This accelerates the viewing time when these pages are reaccessed, as well as enabling the user to browse them offline (i.e. without being connected to the Internet), since the information comes directly from the hard disk and not from the original server. In order to ensure that the last version of the page offered by the server is displayed, the cache can be cleaned or the page refreshed.
In general, the amount of cache memory can be defined by the user, and it is important to get this right, because if a disk is too full, it can crash if the cache is set too high. Some *ISPs* keep the pages most visited by their clients in cache, so the display speed is further enhanced.

CAD (Computer Aided Design)
Computer programs for designing objects in 2D and 3D. Very commonly used in architecture, town planning, engineering and design of all kinds of products. One of the best known is AutoCAD.

Canarie (Canada's Advanced Internet Development Organisation)

CANARIE INC.

A Canadian non-profit-making organisation, based in Ottawa, Ontario, which is dedicated to the acceleration of future development of the Internet in Canada. It is the Canadian section of INTERNET2, in operation since 1993, and it develops the fibre-optic networking technology DWDM (Dense Wavelength Division Multiplexed), capable of transmitting 40 Gigabits. The fibre optics increase the bandwidth, enabling 32 different colours of laser light

to be conducted simultaneously. Canarie directs the technical design of fibre-optic networking. The consortium includes Bell Canada, *Cisco* systems, JDS Fitel, Newbridge Networks and Northern Telecom Inc. (Nortel).
Its website is www.canarie.ca.
See INTERNET2

carbon copy
See CC:

cascade
Consecutive reply mails upon the arrival of a message from *USENET* newsgroups.

cascading style sheets (CSS)
A facility to add style (font, colours, etc.) in web documents.

cc:, to cc: (carbon copy)
A common e-mail facility which enables a message to be copied to other recipients. 'Carbon copy' refers to the old carbon paper that enabled a copy of the original to be made on a typewriter. On the Internet, copies of messages can be sent to as many individuals as required by typing their e-mail addresses in the 'cc:' space.
See BCC:

CCITT (Comité Consultatif International de Telegraphie et Telephonie or International Telegraph and Telephone Consultative Committee)
French acronym of the International Group for Standardisation, forming part of the ITU (International Telecommunication Union) of the United Nations. Responsible for making global technical changes in the telecommunication market. Of particular relevance is the 'V series', which establishes standards in commercial modems.

CD-ROM (Compact Disk Read Only Memory)
Storage system that can contain up to 650 MB of data; at present, the most widely used system for distributing software.

Cello
Browser for Windows from the Cornell Law School, no longer in use due to the strength gained by Microsoft and Netscape browsers.

Cerf, Vincent
President of the *ISOC (Internet Society)* and one of the inventors of *TCP/IP (Transmission Control Protocol/Internet Protocol)*, which allows computers communicate with each other on the Internet.

CERN (Conseil Européen pour la Recherche Nucléaire)

European organisation, located in Geneva, Switzerland, that founded the World Wide Web. In this organisation, Dr *Tim Berners-Lee* developed *HTTP (hypertext transfer protocol)* in 1991.
Its website is www.cern.ch.

CERT (Computer Emergency Response Team)
An organisation created in November 1988 by *DARPA (Defence Applied Research Projects Agency)*, a United States Defence Department agency, after the 'Morris Worm' event, when ten per cent of computers connected to the Internet were affected. Its purpose is to find solutions to problems related to computing security events involving Internet servers, as well as to perform studies designed for improving security in present systems.
It also offers telephone and e-mail support services, maintaining up-to-date e-mail lists and an *anonymous FTP* serv er where documents and tools related to security are stored.
In April 2000, the Carnegie Mellon University developed the CMISS (Carnegie Mellon Institute for Survivable Systems), of which the CERT is now a member.
It may be visited at www.cert.org

certificate
A guarantee of the validity of a *public key*. It is very important to be completely sure that the public key being used to verify a signature or to encrypt text real ly belongs to the person it is thought to belong to.
It would be unwise to encrypt confidential text with the public key of somebody who is not the intended recipient. If so, any individual who owns the public key used to encrypt it would be able to access it.
Likewise, if the public key of somebody who could be taken for somebody else is used without being detected, a signature could be considered valid and appear to be created by somebody who is not really who he/she pretends to be.
To work appropriately, certificates include the following fields:
- an identifier of the individual who owns the certificate;
- another identifier of the individual who ensures its validity, which will be a certification authority;
- the start and end date of the certificate's validity period. After the validity date, the key must not be used to encrypt or sign;
- a certificate identifier or a serial number, which will be unique;
- the public key belonging to somebody who appears in the first identifier's field, the owner and user of the electronic certificate;
- the signature of the certification authority in all the certificate fields, which ensures its authenticity.

The certificate provides authentication to the participants, and provides the transaction with integrity, confidentiality and non-refusal.
The process of obtaining a certificate can be described as follows:
Charles, both to encrypt a message and to verify a signature in a document by John, must have John's public key. The way to obtain this public key is to get an electronic certificate from John. When Charles has John's certificate and the public key from the certification authority that ensures its validity, he can safely get the public key, without worrying that it does not belong to John. To get John's certificate, Charles must have access to the di-

rectory and ask for the certificate to download it and use it. For Charles, another way of getting the certificate is by receiving a message from John that includes the certificate. The certificate travels generally with a digital signature.
See CERTIFICATE, CERTIFICATION AUTHORITY, ENCRYPTION, DIGITAL SIGNATURE, CRYPTOGRAPHY

certification authority
An organisation or firm that issues digital certificates designed to ensure the identity of the owners who use them for electronic transactions or in areas related to the digital signature.
See CERTIFICATE, ENCRYPTION, DIGITAL SIGNATURE, CRYPTOGRAPHY

CGI (Common Gateway Interface)
An interface that defines how a web server communicates with other software within the same computer and vice versa. The CGI program collects data from the web server and uses it, for example, to search databases, generate passwords, process forms and write e-mail messages. This function thus increases the website functionality. Programs must be written in Perl, *C, C++* or *Java*.
Maybe the clearest and the most used example is performing a search on the Internet. When a term is typed into the web-page search box, a personalised page is received with the search results from the web server. Another familiar example is the 'you are the visitor number xx', which appears on many websites. This information is updated by means of a CGI when entering the page and acknowledging a new hit.

cgi-bin
A directory on the web server where the CGI programs are stored. The 'bin' suffix comes from 'binary', since most programs were formerly referred to as binary programs.

chain letter
E-mails which ask the user to forward them to other people. For many people, this is a form of *spam* between acquaintances.
The messages may be of different kinds:
- those that offer the opportunity to get rich quick;
- those to aid specific causes by sending protest messages to certain firms, public agencies or national representatives, as well as to other people who will also protest;
- those appealing to users' humanitarian natures and request assistance for sick people;
- those promising good luck/threatening back luck to the user if they do/don't pass the message on;
- those warning of the appearance of a virus.

Some of these e-mails are bona fide messages, but more often than not they are hoaxes that should be ignored.

channel
See CHAT ROOM

chat (Conversational Hypertext Access Technology)
One of the most used and widespread services on the Internet. Chat software allows two or more users to maintain a conversation in real time, writing messages and sending them via the Internet, so other users can see them as they are

produced. These messages appear staggered on the screen and allow users to hold a conversation similar to a real one. Conversations take place in *chat rooms* or on the *IRC* channels. Chats allow users to have conversations with friends, relatives or even strangers (this is the most common) around the world, and is the modern version of the radio ham.

To access chats, it is usually necessary to have a name (a real one or an alias) which is used in conversations. Alternatively, special software must be downloaded. Some chat programs support voice as well as file exchange (photos and pictures), others allow the user to appear as a fictional character (with the appearance of a drawing or photo) in a virtual-reality environment, such as a landscape or a room. With the increase in telecommunications speed, chats with video and sound will become commonplace.

In websites with chat services, users often have to select the kind of room where the chat takes place. These rooms are sorted by subjects (friendship, trips, sex, sports, etc.). Some chats have become famous where celebrities (politicians, like Bill Clinton, movie stars, singers, etc.) participate and answer users' questions.

See AVATAR, IRC

chat history

Transcription of a *chat* session, i.e. all the interactions between the conversation participants.

chat room

Virtual rooms where *chats* take place, usually sorted by subjects (young people, my city, etc.). There are also private rooms where users can chat with other people without the messages being read by anybody else. Also referred to as channels.

See CHAT

chat server

A server that allows communication among people around the world in a similar way to a real conversation. An example is *Internet Relay Chat (IRC)*.

chatting

Having conversations in a *chat*.

check box, checkbox

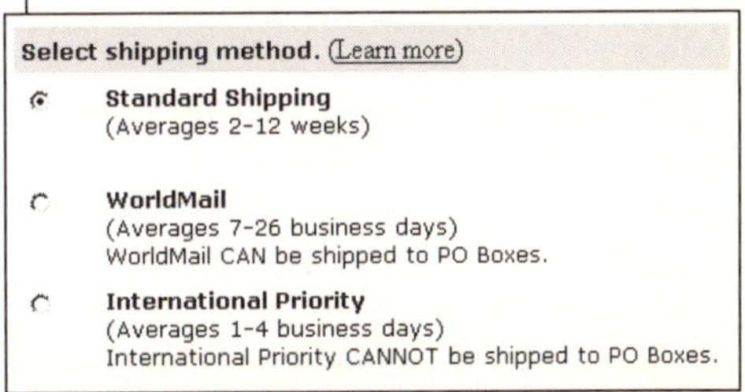

On Internet forms, check boxes allow users to make selections, thereby customising the forms. For example, when filling in a shopping page, there may be three delivery options (e.g. 24 hours, 48 hours or one week) which can be selected by clicking on the relevant check box. The example shows Amazon's shipment options.

See E-FORM

churn

The loss of users from a service. Churn usually increases with the appearance of aggressive competitors or when the promotional time of a service ends and the client prefers not to use it or to look for another option.

Cisco

The leading company in the world providing Internet networks. Cisco's technology connects people, computing equipment and all kinds of computer networks.

click

1 The process of clicking with the mouse to visit another location.
2 Especially in advertising, clicking on a banner to access the requested page.

The term *click through* is also used, although this term implies that the user has received the page in question.
See CLICK RATE

click-and-mortar

Informal term for companies that do business on the Internet and in the real world. Traditional companies are called 'brick-and-mortar' businesses. Companies which operate in both spheres combine the 'click' of browsing with the traditional 'mortar', maximising their coverage.

click rate

Related to *click*, this is the percentage of users who click an advertisement banner to access the advertiser's web page. For example, if 100 users see an advertisement banner at the top of a page and two of them click it, the click rate of the advertisement is two per cent.
With the exception of some very aggressive advertisements (e.g. 'click here and you will receive a present'), the click rate is usually very low - one per cent on average and rarely exceeding five per cent. It also refers to the number of ad views resulting in *click through*.

click stream

The click sequence (path) a user performs through Internet pages. This data allows the advertisers and website owners to improve the communication with the users and optimise the ads and contents.

click through

Term closely related to *click*, referring to access to a web page generated by clicking on an advertising banner located on another page. Usually measured as a percentage ('click through ratio').

clickable image

Graphic included in an *HMTL* page that is associated with other information and allows users to click on it to perform another function, e.g. link to another page. For example, clicking on an image of a mailbox can enable users to send e-mail to the owner of the website.

clickable image map, clickable map

A more sophisticated *clickable image*, since it allows the same image to have different areas where users can click and access other areas.

For example, by clicking on different areas of a city map, the user may be able to access information on monuments, streets, shops, etc.

client
A computing program that allows a computer to access a server to request the information it requires (*client/server* relationship). An example is the use of a browser to request information on the Internet (Internet client).

client/server
The relationship established between programs in different computers within a network. The server provides services and contents and the client uses them in remote mode.

Cnet

Portal owned by CNET Networks, Inc., specialising in information about computing, the Internet and technologies. One of the most complete portals in the world. Its website is www.cnet.com.

.co
The domain suffix used in the United Kingdom to represent companies. It usually follows the company's name and precedes the country domain. For example, the Amazon store's address in the United Kingdom is www.amazon.co.uk.

coax, coaxial cable
A kind of cable that includes two copper conductors, one inside the other, isolated internally and externally by a plastic isolator. It is the kind of cable used for television antennae or for *Ethernet* connections.

COBOL (Common Business-Oriented Language)
A programing language developed in the sixties by the United States Defence Department and by several computing companies.

.com
One of the suffixes that can be chosen when requesting a domain registration. Websites using this domain name usually have a commercial purpose. It is the most widespread suffix on the Internet, because it is universally understood and easy to obtain. An example is www.atkeaney.com.

CommerceNet

An American organisation created in California in April 1994 and made up of more than 600 companies and with representatives in many countries. It provides an international forum to promote, encourage and enhance the use of the Internet for electronic commerce through the support of its members, banks, telecommu-

nication companies, *ISPs*, software and service companies, etc.
Its website is www.commercenet.com.

Common Business-Oriented Language
See COBOL

Common Gateway Interface
See CGI

communications program/software
A program used to establish communication and to share information with other computers, usually by means of a *modem* and a telephone line.

Communicator, Netscape Communicator
Free browser formerly known as Netscape Navigator, provided by the company *Netscape*. One of the two most popular browsers on the Internet (the other being Microsoft Internet *Explorer*).
See NETSCAPE.

.comp (computer newsgroup)
A superior category of the *USENET* newsgroups dedicated to computing.
Other newsgroup categories are .alt (alternative), .news, .sci (science), .talk, .biz (business), .misc (miscellaneous), .rec (recreational) and .soc (social).
Access to these newsgroups may be gained through most Internet browsers.
See NEWSGROUPS

compressed file
A file whose size has been reduced using one of the specific programs for *compression*. This is especially useful on the Internet when transferring documents attached to e-mails. The best-known compression programs are *PKZIP* (in DOS systems), *WinZip* and *StuffIt*, and the best-known compression formats are .zip, .arj and .tar.

compression
Used to reduce the size of files for easier storage or transfer. On the Internet, this is especially useful for transferring files by e-mail, since the low speed of transmission makes it sensible to reduce the size of files as much as possible. Some compression programs involve a loss of data, others do not. Decompression software is needed to be able to open compressed files.
Common examples of compression software are *WinZip*, *PKZIP* and the *UNIX* facility. Compressed files usually have the letter 'z' in their file extension to indicate that they are compressed, for example 'text.zip'.
There are also compression formats for images, such as JPEG, as well as others for sound and video.
See COMPRESSION PROGRAM

compression formats
There are a many programs used for compressing or decompressing files which store the files in their own formats. Some examples of compression-format extensions: .zip, .arj, .lzh and .tar.

compression program
A program used to reduce the size of files and thereby reduce the space occupied

on the hard disk. This also means files can be sent more quickly by e-mail. Some of the best-known programs are *WinZip*, *PKZIP* and *StuffIt*. Compressed files usually have the letter 'z' in their file extension to indicate that they are compressed, for example 'text.zip'. The compression software also performs decompression or expansion.
There are also compression programs for images, such as JPEG, as well as others for sound and video.
See COMPRESSION

CompuServe
Also known as CIS (CompuServe Information Service), this was one of the first and most famous paying services providing access to the Internet. It was taken over by *AOL*.

Computer Aided Design
See CAD

Computer Emergency Response Team
See CERT

congestion
The situation on the Internet that occurs when there is a high number of users logged on at one time. It causes a slowing in data transmission because the amount of data transmitted is higher than the transmission capacity of the Internet.
See BOTTLENECK

connect time
The amount of time a user is online, using a free or paying *Internet Service Provider (ISP)*. It is measured in hours or minutes of connection, and the telephone connection during this period is paid for on a pro-rata basis or a fixed monthly rate with unlimited use (occasionally on a fixed-time basis).

connection
A communication established between two computers to exchange information. Also defined as the communication between a client computer and a server by means of authorisation.

content
The sum of texts, images, sound, data, video, graphics, etc. on a web page.

Conversational Hypertext Access Technology
See CHAT

cookie

A file containing very little information, sent by a website and stored on the user's hard disk. Cookies allow the website to identify the user, follow his/her path during the visit and build up an individual profile so that more customised information can be provided. It also permits the user's operating system to identify the last page visited, recognise the browser used, save the log information, access a website, generate the shopping cart, etc. Each time the same website is accessed, the cookies let the server know if that user has been there before. This can be useful in advertisement areas, since it allows advertisers to send different ads without duplication and even to customise them according to the user profile. Cookies also store the access key log and user identification for many websites, saving the user from typing them in each time or going through the complete identification process.

Many users consider cookies as an invasion to their privacy. For this reason, most browsers flash up an alert when a cookie is received, giving the user the option to reject it. Cookies cannot have access to other areas of the user's computer (hard disk), nor can they gain access to e-mail addresses or other personal data. Each website issues its own cookie, which cannot be accessed by others.

The process is as follows:

- A cookie is sent when a website is first accessed.
- The cookie is stored in a directory in the browser in the form of a text file. Many cookies have an expiry date, and some of them expire when the user logs off the browser.
- When the page is re-accessed, the cookie is checked.
- The user is identified, enabling services to be customised or information about the user to be retained.

Cookies are generally written in *CGI* scripts, although they sometimes use *JavaScript*.

If the directory where the cookies are stored is accessed and one of them is opened, it will look something like the one from Amazon on the previous page.

cookie files

The directory where cookies sent by websites are stored.

See COOKIES

cookie suppressers

A facility that prevents *cookies* entering into a computer.

cost per click

The amount that the advertising agency or the website itself charges the advertising company for the number of clicks on its ads (banner). It is an alternative to charging for the number of times a page is downloaded, which ensures that the ad on the page was seen.

cost per thousand page views/ impressions, cost per thousand

Cost for viewing 1000 ads. A term used in traditional advertising and Internet media to measure the price of advertisements.

cost per visit (CPV)

The amount that has to be paid for each visitor accessing the website via a banner placed in another website.

counter, hit counter

A graphic, usually similar to a car milometer, that indicates the number of times a page has been accessed. It is usually placed on the home page of a website (mainly non-commercial). A high number indi-

cates that a website has been visited by many people, but this information should be taken with a pinch of salt, as some sites have counters which start at a very high number or which constantly increase the total rather than adding to it only when the site is visited. Programs performing this function are usually free and can be downloaded from many sites on the Internet. This also applies to visit-analysis programs on websites.

country code
Country codes are used as a domain. For example, Spain uses the code '.es' (www.miempresa.es) and Germany uses '.de' (e.g. www.wirtschaft.de). Country codes are always composed of two letters set down by the *ISO*.
See DOMAIN

CPU (Central Processing Unit)
The chip that manages the operating system and programs of a computer.

CPV
See COST PER VISIT

cracker
In Internet argot, a malicious person who passes without authorisation through a company's computing security systems to gain access to a certain information, steal it or destroy it. Crackers should not be confused with *hackers*, as the latter lack the former's destructive tendancies and do not like to be associated with them.
See HACKER

crawler
See SPIDER

cross-post, cross-posting
To send the same message simultaneously to multiple *newsgroups* or mail lists. To abuse this practice or to send trivial messages is considered to be a breach of Internet etiquette (*Netiquette*).

cryptography, crypto
The science of encrypting data in such a way that only authorised people are able to decrypt it using the appropriate key. Algorithms are usually used to encrypt the information. One of the best known on the Internet is *PGP*.

See CERTIFICATE, CERTIFICATION AUTHORITY, ENCRYPTION, DIGITAL SIGNATURE, CRYPTOGRAPHY, PGP.

CUSEMEE/CU-SeeMee
A free program used to perform low-speed videoconferencing on the Internet. Two or more users are allowed.

cyber
From the Greek word 'kiberman' meaning 'to govern'.
It is used as a prefix to describe subjects related to the Internet, such as *cyberspace*, cybernaut or cybernewspaper. In the Internet community, using this term is considered characteristic of *newbies*.

cybercafé
A coffee shop where Internet facilities are provided via multiple terminals. Customers are usually charged per hour of use, and peripheral services (e.g. fax, e-mail, printers) are also provided. Cybercafés are becoming more and more popular and can be found in almost every city around the world.

cyberpunk
1 A science-fiction sub-genre, inspired by novels by American authors and based on societies of the future, the principal exponent being William Gibson.
2 A lifestyle characterised by computer games, Internet browsing and a certain anarchic attitude.

cybersex
Any kind of sexual activity on the Internet.

cybermall
See E-MALL

cyberspace
A term coined by the American science-fiction writer William Ford Gibson (born 1948) in his first novel 'Neuromancer', published in 1984, to describe the future in computing with an advanced computer network. This novel established a new trend and obtained three prestigious science-fiction awards.
Users are described as being in cyberspace when surfing the Internet. The term is also used to describe all the information resources available via a computer.
Other terms used in a similar way are *Internet*, *World Wide Web*, WWW, triple W or *Information Superhighway*.

cybersquatting
An extension of the word 'squatter', i.e. a person who illegally occupies non-occupied land or housing. On the Internet, it describes the action of registering domains with the purpose of selling them afterwards to companies that wish to use them. There have been a number of cases of domain registration of well-known company names by Internet squatters, who aim to sell them for very large amounts of money.

daemon
A UNIX term applied to the background process that performs certain tasks in predefined moments or before certain actions. The best-known daemons are HTTP Daemon (HTTPD), smtp daemon, telnetd (telnet) or ftpd (ftp).

DARPA (Defence Advanced Research Projects Agency)

United States Defence Department Agency that is responsible for many of the present concepts on the Internet. It was created in 1958 as a first response to the launch of the Soviet Sputnik. Its website is www.darpa.mil.
See DARPA and ARPANet.

Data Encryption Key (DEK)
A key used to encrypt or decrypt messages. This can only be done with a key, so its confidentiality is guaranteed.

Data Encryption Standard (DES)
One of the most popular encryption systems in the Internet. It was developed by the US National Institute of Standards and Technology.

data traffic
The amount of information that flows through a network. On the Internet, it refers to the number of *TCP/IP* packets being transmitted. When the number of packets requested simultaneously from a server is very high, the delivery speed is reduced.

database
A structured file that contains data, images, films and other documents that have been sorted into fields. It allows access by means of different levels and searching systems. From the point of view of the Internet user, it allows access to large amounts of ordered information. For example, when a search on one of the specialist websites is requested, it gives access to a database that provides information.

DDN (Defence Data Network)
The global communication network of the United States Defence Department that connects military facilities. It consists of MILNET, parts of the Internet and networks that are not within the Internet environment.

dead link
A link which fails because the page in question has disappeared or the server is out of service.

decompression
See COMPRESSION

decryption
The procedure of opening an encoded message and making it legible.
See CERTIFICATION AUTHORITY, ENCRYPTION, CRYPTOGRAPHY, DIGITAL SIGNATURE, PGP.

dedicated line
A telephone line between two computers. In the case of the Internet, it is a direct and permanent connection.

Defence Advanced Research Projects Agency
See DARPA

Defence Data Network
See DDN

DEK
See Data Encryption Key

delay
See latency

Delphi
Besides being a development language, Delphi is known in the Internet environment as being one of the first information providers and ISPs in the United States.

DES
See Data Encryption Standard

design tools
See tools, design

DHTML
See HTML, dynamic

dial-up, dial-up access
A temporary connection via modem between a computer and an *ISP* using analogue telephone lines or *ISDN* that allows access to the Internet. It is the most common means of access to the Internet, especially for domestic users.

dial-up account
The account established with an *ISP* to enable users to connect to the Internet via a telephone line.

dial-up service/access provider
A company that provides access to the Internet through a dial-up connection. These companies usually charge a fee, although there are also free services.

dialer
A program that establishes the connection between a computer and the Internet.

dialog box
Message that appears on the screen asking about a particular action. For example, when downloading files from a website, a message may appear asking if the files should be saved to the hard disk or displayed immediately.

digerati
'Digital elite', from the Latin 'Literati', referring to experts in the vanguard of the digital revolution.

digital
The opposite of analogue. It describes the technology that generates and processes data in two kinds of states, positive and non-positive. The positive state is represented by the digit 1 and the non-positive by the digit 0. Digital data is represented as a chain of 0s and 1s, named *bits*, and a group of eight bits is equivalent to one *byte*. These digits are used to represent text, data, images, audio, etc. Thus, a digitalised image con-

sists of a series of 0s and 1s that is interpreted by the corresponding software, represents an image on the computer screen and allows its transmission, storage or modification.
See BIT, BYTE

digital signature
The best way to understand this concept is through the explanation provided by the Spanish Certification Agency (ACE): Charles knows John's public key and wishes to receive a signed text, so Charles may be absolutely sure that the text, such as it is received, can only be sent by John. Although a third party tries to manipulate the text, Charles would detect, when verifying the signature, that the text received is not the same John sent. Also, Charles could prove to third parties that the text in his hands was sent by John, and John would not be able to deny it (non refusal). John signs the text using his private key, which is known only by him, and sends Charles the signed text. Charles receives the text and through John's public key, known by everybody, checks that the text's signature is correct.
By using this technique, anyone who knows John's public key could check any text signed by him, that only he is capable of signing with his private key.
More on this can be found at ACE's website at www.ace.es
See CERTIFICATE, CERTIFICATION AUTHORITY, ENCRYPTION, DIGITAL SIGNATURE, CRYPTOGRAPHY

direct connection
A direct connection between a computer and the Internet, without the need for an intermediate server. It is much faster than the dial-up connection and requires an *IP address*.

directory, directory service
Directories depend on people to create, index and update their listings, which are sorted in categories and subcategories. The main difference between a *search engine* and a directory is that the directory usually does not use a *spider* or robot. This means that a directory will not list a website if it is not registered. Directories are divided into categories, and the *URL* must be sent to the most appropriate categories. Classification in categories makes it easy

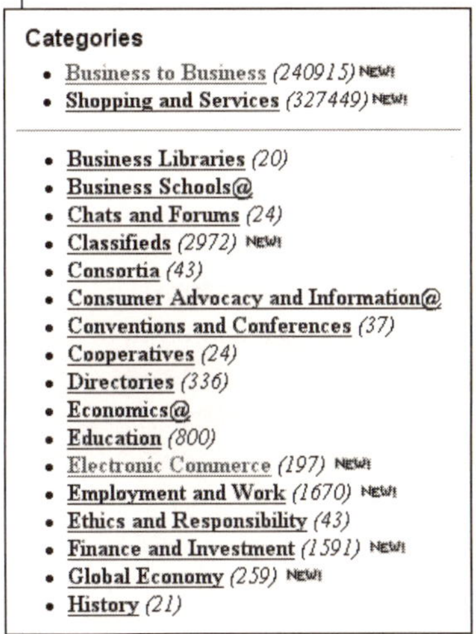

to find the websites that are being sought. A typical case is Yahoo. The example above shows one of Yahoo's directories.

DirectX
Microsoft technology that works under Windows 95 and Windows NT and consists of a group of *APIs (application pro-*

gram interfaces) that allows programers to access computer graphic and audio facilities more directly. In this way, dynamic websites can be created with a high multimedia content, such as 3D, graphics, video and audio.

discussion board
An Internet forum where an exchange of opinions take place about certain subjects.

discussion group
An area inside the *USENET* dedicated to a particular subject, to a newsgroup. Messages about this subject are exchanged within this group.

distributed database
A group of databases located in different areas that work as a unit from the user's point of view.

DNS (Domain Name System)
The mechanism used in the Internet to translate domain names into addresses. It is a hierarchical, static system, hosted in duplicate on a certain number of servers on the Internet. Most DNS servers contain a database where the names are cross-referenced to their digital addresses, and which is regularly updated. Other computers send these servers requests to transform a name address into the digital equivalent in order to correctly route the page request.
Each computer on the Internet has a unique *IP address* consisting of digits. DNS allows users to locate remote servers by their domain names instead of digital IP addresses, which are not easy to remember. If the requested DNS is not found, it will ask other DNS servers to try to locate it. If this is not successful, an error message appears in the browser screen. For example, www.sprint.com corresponds to the *IP number* 208.25.106.10. Writing either of these addresses (digital or alphabetical) will display the Sprint page. The best-known DNS suffixes have two or three letters, such as:

.com domain for a commercial entity
.co domain for a limited company (always followed by a country code)
.edu domain for a university or educational institution
.gov domain for a government organisation in the United States
.mil domain for military use in the United States
.net domain for organisations on the Internet
.org domain for non-profit-making organisations

There is also a two-letter domain suffix for each country. For example, '.es' is the domain for Spain and '.fr' is for France.
See IP ADDRESS, IP NUMBER

DNSO (Domain Name Supporting Organisation)
The control group for the standards relating to the domain name system. It counsels the *ICANN (Internet Corporation for Assigned Names and Numbers)* directors. Its website is www.dnso.org.

domain, domain name
The term used to describe the name associated with an IP numerical address. In an address like www.atkearney.com, it in-

dicates the domain used by the company A.T. Kearney: 'www' indicates World Wide Web, 'atkearney' is the company's name and '.com' indicates that it is a company or business. Each section of the domain is separated by a dot from the preceding name. The domains are unique, and there cannot be duplications on the Internet. The domain is also used for e-mail address, such as watson@atkearney.com.

First-level domains are administered by the control agency *InterNIC*. Once registered, they are owned by their registrar. This system has caused the registering of domains with the purpose of being sold later to the companies that should have used these domains, since they represent the company's name. The organisation *IANA (Internet Assigned Numbers Authority)* holds responsibility for domain names.

The best-known generic first-level domains are:

.com domain for a commercial entity
.co domain for a limited company (always followed by a country code)
.edu domain for a university or educational institution
.gov domain for a government organisation in the United States
.mil domain for military use in the United States
.net domain for organisations on the Internet
.org domain for non-profit-making organisations

Since the number of free domains is now becoming scarce, new first-level domain names are being established, such as: .firm, .store, .web, .arts, .rec, .nom and .info. In many cases, a website does not have its own domain name and is included under another domain. These are called subdomains, for example http://sunsite.ee/animals. This is usually because registering a domain has an initial cost and an annual maintenance fee, and many companies and individuals prefer to use subdomains.

The domain corresponds to a series of numbers, the *IP numbers*. It is easier to remember a domain name than a numerical code.

To register a domain name ending .com, .net or .org, it is necessary to request it from one of the multiple Internet companies that provide this service; prices are variable according to a particular company, and the data is made public through *Whois*. The initial validity period of the registration is two years, then annual thereafter.

In addition, each country has its own two-letter extension (except the United States, where the domain system started). These are called ccTLDs, or country code top-level domains. Thus, '.es' is Spain, '.de' is Germany, '.jp' is Japan, etc. Domains for most countries in the world are in the following list:

.ac Ascension Island
.ad Andorra
.ae United Arab Emirates
.af Afghanistan
.ag Antigua and Barbuda
.ai Anguilla
.al Albania
.am Armenia
.an Netherlands Antilles
.ao Angola
.aq Antarctica
.ar Argentina

.as	American Samoa
.at	Austria
.au	Australia
.aw	Aruba
.az	Azerbaijan
.ba	Bosnia and Herzegovinia
.bb	Barbados
.bd	Bangladesh
.be	Belgium
.bf	Burkina Faso
.bg	Bulgaria
.bh	Bahrain
.bi	Burundi
.bj	Benin
.bm	Bermuda
.bn	Brunei
.bo	Bolivia
.br	Brazil
.bs	Bahamas
.bt	Bhutan
.bv	Bouvet Island
.bw	Botswana
.by	Belarus
.bz	Belize
.ca	Canada
.cc	Cocos Islands or Keeling Islands
.cf	Central African Republic
.cg	Congo
.ch	Switzerland
.ci	Côte D'Ivoire, Ivory Coast
.ck	Cook Islands
.cl	Chile
.cm	Cameroon
.cn	China
.co	Colombia (and first-level domain for some companies)
.cr	Costa Rica
.cs	Czechoslovakia (no longer in existence – see .cz)
.cu	Cuba
.cv	Cape Verde
.cx	Christmas Island
.cy	Cyprus
.cz	Czech Republic
.de	Germany
.dj	Djibouti
.dk	Denmark
.dm	Dominica
.do	Dominican Republic
.dz	Algeria
.ec	Ecuador
.ee	Estonia
.eg	Egypt
.eh	Western Sahara
.er	Eritrea
.es	Spain
.et	Ethiopia
.fi	Finland
.fj	Fiji
.fk	Falkland Islands/Malvinas
.fm	Micronesia
.fo	Faroe Islands
.fr	France
.fx	Metropolitan France
.ga	Gabon
.gb	Great Britain
.gd	Grenada
.ge	Georgia (formerly a Republic of the USSR)
.gf	French Guiana
.gg	Guernsey
.gh	Ghana
.gi	Gibraltar
.gl	Greenland
.gm	Gambia
.gn	Guinea
.gp	Guadeloupe
.gq	Equatorial Guinea
.gr	Greece
.gs	South Georgia and South

	Sandwich Islands
.gt	Guatemala
.gu	Guam
.gw	Guinea-Bissau
.gy	Guyana
.hk	Hong Kong
.hm	Heard and McDonald Islands
.hn	Honduras
.hr	Croatia/Hrvatska
.ht	Haiti
.hu	Hungary
.id	Indonesia
.ie	Ireland
.il	Israel
.im	Isle of Man
.in	India
.io	British Indian Ocean Territory
.iq	Iraq
.ir	Iran
.is	Iceland
.it	Italy
.je	Jersey
.jm	Jamaica
.jo	Jordan
.jp	Japan
.ke	Kenya
.kg	Kyrgyzstan
.kh	Cambodia
.ki	Kiribati
.km	Comoros
.kn	Saint Kitts and Nevis
.kp	North Korea
.kr	South Korea
.kw	Kuwait
.ky	Cayman Islands
.kz	Kazakhstan
.la	Laos
.lb	Lebanon
.lc	Saint Lucia
.li	Liechtenstein
.lk	Sri Lanka
.lr	Liberia
.ls	Lesotho
.lt	Lithuania
.lu	Luxembourg
.lv	Latvia
.ly	Libya
.ma	Morocco
.mc	Monaco
.md	Moldova
.mg	Madagascar
.mh	Marshall Islands
.mk	Macedonia
.ml	Mali
.mm	Myanmar
.mn	Mongolia
.mo	Macau
.mp	Northern Mariana Islands
.mq	Martinique
.mr	Mauritania
.ms	Montserrat
.mt	Malta
.mu	Mauritius
.mv	Maldives
.mw	Malawi
.mx	Mexico
.my	Malaysia
.mz	Mozambique
.na	Namibia
.nc	New Caledonia
.ne	Niger
.nf	Norfolk Island
.ng	Nigeria
.ni	Nicaragua
.nl	The Netherlands
.no	Norway
.np	Nepal
.nr	Nauru
.nt	Neutral Zone
.nu	Niue

.nz	New Zealand
.om	Oman
.pa	Panama
.pe	Peru
.pf	French Polynesia
.pg	Papua New Guinea
.ph	Philippines
.pk	Pakistan
.pl	Poland
.pm	St. Pierre et Miquelon
.pn	Pitcairn
.pr	Puerto Rico
.ps	Palestine
.pt	Portugal
.pw	Palau
.py	Paraguay
.qa	Qatar
.re	Reunion
.ro	Romania
.ru	Russian Federation/Russia
.rw	Rwanda
.sa	Saudi Arabia
.sb	Solomon Islands
.sc	Seychelles
.sd	Sudan
.se	Sweden
.sg	Singapore
.sh	Saint Helena
.si	Slovenia
.sj	Svalbard and Jan Mayen Islands
.sk	Slovakia
.sl	Sierra Leone
.sm	San Marino
.sn	Senegal
.so	Somalia
.sr	Surinam
.st	Sao Torme and Principe
.su	former USSR
.sv	El Salvador
.sy	Syria
.sz	Swaziland
.tc	Turks and Caicos Islands
.td	Tchad
.tf	French Southern Territories
.tg	Togo
.th	Thailand
.tj	Tajikistan
.tk	Tokelau
.tm	Turkmenistan
.tn	Tunisia
.to	Tonga
.tp	East Timor
.tr	Turkey
.tt	Trinidad and Tobago
.tv	Tuvalu
.tw	Taiwan
.tz	Tanzania
.ua	Ukraine
.ug	Uganda
.uk	United Kingdom
.um	U.S. Minor Outlying Islands
.uy	Uruguay
.uz	Uzbekistan
.va	Vatican City State
.vc	Saint Vincent and the Grenadines
.ve	Venezuela
.vg	British Virgin Islands
.vi	U.S. Virgin Islands
.vn	Vietnam
.vu	Vanuatu
.wf	Wallis and Futuna Islands
.wg	Western Jordan and Gaza
.ws	Samoa
.ye	Yemen
.yt	Mayotte
.yu	Yugoslavia
.za	South Africa
.zm	Zambia
.zr	Zaire
.zw	Zimbabwe

Domain Name Supporting Organisation
See DNSO

Domain Name System
See DNS

Doom
A very violent virtual-reality game developed in a 3D world. With the use of the Internet, this game has increased its popularity, since it allows multiple players around the world to play simultaneously.

dot address, dotted decimal notation, dotted address notation
A method for writing *IP addresses* in the format 5.5.5.5, where each of the four numbers represents one *byte*.
See IP NUMBER

download, downloading
Data transfer from a remote server to a personal computer via the Internet using a browser or *FTP*. The opposite process is referred to as uploading (i.e the action of sending local files to be copied onto a remote server).
Care must be taken when downloading to avoid importing viruses onto the hard disk. It is therefore inadvisable to download from unknown or uncertain sites. A wide variety of things can be downloaded from the Internet, including games, software, audio, video, documents, etc., many of which are free of charge.

DSML
An XML language for directory services.

DVD
Digital videodisk, a new kind of disk which looks similar to the CD-ROM introduced by Philips and Sony in 1995 and is capable of storing up to 4.7 *Gigabytes* of data or files of high-definition digital video.

dynamic HTML (DHTML)
A new generation of *HTML* that allows multimedia and customised dynamic content which describes how text and images must be displayed in a web page. The creators of HTML content prepare the pages once and reuse them for other web pages. The pages react to the users' requests by offering contents that change each time they are displayed. It has been developed by Netscape and the *W3C* (World Wide Web Consortium) and is based on HTML and *Java* standards.

dynamic IP addressing
A numerical *IP address* that is variable. Each time a user connects to the Internet, a variable or different IP address is allocated. Some ISPs offer a fixed IP allocation to their users, although this service has a high cost because of the lack of addresses available.
See ISP

dynamic web page
See WEB PAGES, DYNAMIC

e-
A contraction of 'electronic' very commonly used as a prefix on the Internet, for example, *e-commerce*, *e-business*.

e-business (electronic business)
Business performed between companies on the Internet. Electronic commerce is a part of electronic business, as well as marketing and advertising.

e-cash
Electronic money used on the Internet as a substitute for real money.

e-commerce
See ELECTRONIC COMMERCE

e-form, eform, electronic form

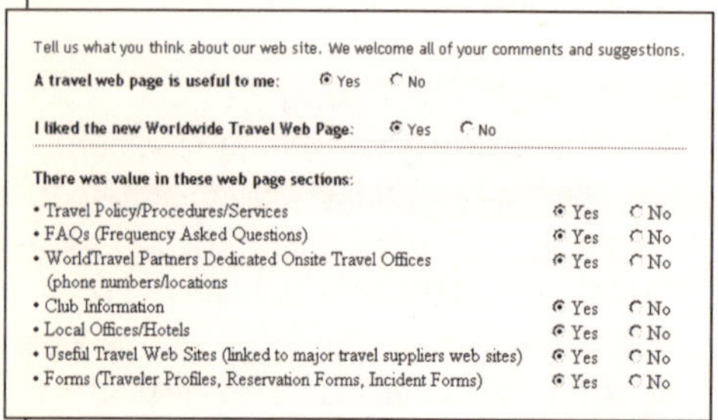
Tell us what you think about our web site. We welcome all of your comments and suggestions.

A travel web page is useful to me: ◉ Yes ○ No

I liked the new Worldwide Travel Web Page: ◉ Yes ○ No

There was value in these web page sections:

- Travel Policy/Procedures/Services ◉ Yes ○ No
- FAQs (Frequency Asked Questions) ◉ Yes ○ No
- WorldTravel Partners Dedicated Onsite Travel Offices (phone numbers/locations ◉ Yes ○ No
- Club Information ◉ Yes ○ No
- Local Offices/Hotels ◉ Yes ○ No
- Useful Travel Web Sites (linked to major travel suppliers web sites) ◉ Yes ○ No
- Forms (Traveler Profiles, Reservation Forms, Incident Forms) ◉ Yes ○ No

A questionnaire, order form, information request form, etc. that may be filled in and sent over the Internet. These forms generally have areas to include text and *check boxes* that can be checked to select different options. They can be used for shopping in a store, subscribing to certain information (e.g. magazines, newspapers, bulletins), requesting information about a product or even, within an *Intranet*, substituting interdepartmental paper documents.
One of the most common examples is when users are requested to supply their e-mail addresses for companies to keep them informed about their products, etc.
See CHECK BOX

e-mail, electronic mail, mail
The computing version of traditional postal mail (called '*snail mail*' or 'snail' by US users). The similarities between the two systems are:
- addresses are used to identify individuals, such as alvaro@atkearney.es.
- there is an area in which the message is written (paper/screen)
- other items can be included with the main message, e.g. documents, video, audio, images, etc.
- messages are entrusted to a postal service for delivery (postman/modem and telephone line).

E-mail offers many advantages compared to traditional mail:
- Speed: in a few seconds, messages can be received from anywhere around the world.
- Cost: the outlay is limited to the cost of the phone call, usually at local tariff or free, if a free-access service is available.
- Security: information can be encrypted in such a way that only the person to whom the message is sent may read it.
- Duplication: the same mail can be sent to multiple users in a single delivery, with-

out having to write to each one of them individually. Mailing lists (lists containing a number of destination addresses to which mail is sent simultaneously) can be used to facilitate this.

E-mail addresses are usually written in lower case and without gaps, and can be divided into different sections. For example, for the address alvaro@atkearney.es:

- 'alvaro' is the user's name or alias; this can take the form of the full name (sometimes separated by a dot), e.g. 'alvaro.castells' or an abbreviated form (e.g. acastells). Other things that appear in this section of an address can be 'webmaster' (which represents the person responsible for a company's website), 'info' (which indicates a mail address where information requests, etc. can be sent), 'support' (which indicates a technical-support address or some other kind of help) and so on
- @ (usually pronounced 'at') divides the user's name from the server information
- 'atkearney' is the domain name that identifies the server,
- '.es' is the country code that indicates Spain. In other cases, it can be a first-level domain such as .com (commercial), .edu (educational), .mil (military), .gov (government), .org (non-commercial) or .net (network).

Electronic mail usually includes, apart from the message and attachments, the following fields:

- 'To': the address of the person receiving the mail.
- 'From': the address of the person who sends it.
- 'Subject': the subject of the message.
- 'cc': other people being sent a copy of the message.
- 'bcc': other people being sent a copy of the message without the original recipient knowing.

E-mails are transmitted on the Internet by means of the *SMTP* protocol, and the most usual reception protocol is the *POP3* protocol. The IMAP4 protocol is also used. Mail text is usually encrypted as *ASCII* text.

e-mail message

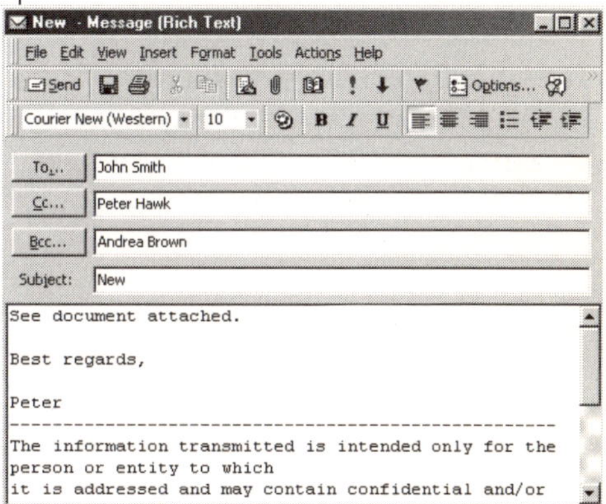

A message sent to one or several people that includes the following fields:

- 'To': the address of the person receiving the mail.
- 'From': the address of the person who sends it.
- 'Subject': the subject of the message.
- 'cc': other people being sent a copy of the message.
- 'bcc': other people being sent a copy of the message without the original recipient knowing.

e-mail server

A computer that controls the e-mail sent and received.

e-mall, electronic mall, virtual mall, cybermall
A group of websites for users to shop. As in the real world, where there are malls made up of specialised shops, the same concept can be found on the Internet.

e-procurement (electronic procurement)
An Internet facility which enables companies to purchase items from product catalogues and organise payment and delivery.

e-tailing (electronic retailing)
A term for Internet commerce between a business and an individual, also called *B2C (business to consumer)*. It does not occur between businesses (*B2B*).

E-World
An online service for Apple Macintosh users that had more than 100,000 members. It no longer exists.

e-zine, 'zine
Magazine distributed over the Internet, that can be exclusively electronic or derive from a paper version (the term is more commonly applied to the former). They are usually devoted to specific areas of interest.

EARN (European Academic and Research Network)
The European arm of *BITNET* that enables academic and research centres to send e-mails and transfer files to each other.
See BITNET

Easter egg
A secret area built into a program by the programer, which can consist of names, jokes, games or anecdotes. Easter eggs are usually deeply hidden within the program, triggered only by an unusual combination of keystrokes, and do not have any concrete function, other than to amuse their creator and see if anyone manages to find them. Their name comes from the traditional Easter-egg hunt and the possibility of finding a surprise inside. They are common in many popular computing programs, such as Excel, FrontPage and Windows, and in an increasing number of websites.

EDI (Electronic Data Interchange)
Electronic data transmission system between businesses which is very widespread in certain areas, such as the automobile and food industries.

EDIFACT (Electronic Data Interchange for Administration, Commerce and Transport)
The international standard that describes *EDI* message syntax.

.edu
A domain suffix which usually corresponds to an educational establishment, university or research institution, for example www.mit.edu (the Massachusetts Institute of Technology), www.stanford.edu (Stanford University in the United States) or www.ie.edu (the Instituto de Empresa in Madrid).
See DOMAIN

EFF (Electronic Frontier Foundation)
A private, non-profit-making organisation founded in California, US, in Ju-

ly 1990, that addresses issues related to privacy, freedom of speech and access to information on the Internet. Its aim is to resolve conflicts and ensure that all kinds of freedom are respected on the Internet. Its website is at www.eff.org

electronic commerce
The performance of commercial operations on the Internet in a similar way to those performed in the real world. For example, when products are bought in an Internet shop and paid for online, this is electronic commerce.

electronic bulletin board
See BBS

Electronic Data Interchange
See EDI

Electronic Data Interchange for Administration, Commerce and Transport
See EDIFACT

electronic form
See E-FORM

Electronic Frontier Foundation
See EFF

electronic mail
See E-MAIL

electronic mall
See E-MALL

electronic procurement
See E-PROCUREMENT

emoticon
A combination of the words 'emotion' and 'icon'. Emoticons are used to express emotions and states of mind over the Internet and sprang up to counteract the impersonal nature of a written message and any misunderstandings that could arise from misreading the tone, especially when users write in a non-native language. They are most frequently used in *e-mail*, *USENET* newsgroups and *chats*. They are composed of different combinations of *ASCII* characters (symbols, letters and numbers from the keyboard), which often show faces with expressions that can be seen better by looking at them sideways. There are hundreds of emoticons, but only some of them are used frequently. The most common are:
:-) smile, happiness
:-(sadness, trouble
8-) smile with glasses
;-) a wink, somewhat happy, just joking
:-o amazement, surprise
Another way of expressing an emotion is by writing everything in UPPER CASE, which is the e-mail equivalent of shouting.

encryption
The process of encrypting valuable and confidential data in such a way that it can only be opened with a key and read (decodified, decrypted) by authorised persons. The key is an algorithm that inverts the encryption process.
Encryption is done by means of certain programs that transform the information

into a bit-code that is difficult to translate. On the Internet, browsers and servers generally use *SSL (Secure Socket Layers)* to protect information linked with payment methods, such as data about credit cards. One of the most commonly used programes is *PGP (Pretty Good Privacy)*.
To decode encrypted documents, computers are used that try to break the code and gain access to information. The more complex an encryption algorithm is, the more difficult it will be to open documents.
Encryption is perhaps best explained by the following example:
John has two keys: a private one and a public one, which are linked. Each of them complements the other one, that is, what is done by the first one is also done by the second one and vice versa. The public key, as the name indicates, is available to everyone and, therefore, anyone could use it. On the other hand, the private key is only known by John, and he is the only one able to use it.
In this example, if Charles knows John's public key, he can send him an encrypted text which only John will be able to read. Even if a third person had the encrypted text, they would find it impossible to read.
Charles encrypts the document with John's public key. John receives the encrypted text and, using his private key, decrypts it, getting the original, legible text.
By using this encryption technique, anybody who has John's public key would be able to send him encrypted text that only John will be able to decrypt with his private key.
See CERTIFICATE, CERTIFICATION AUTHORITY, ENCRYPTION, CRIPTOGRAPHY, DIGITAL SIGNATURE, PGP.

Ethernet
A protocol for *LAN (local area network)* developed by Xerox, Intel and DEC (Digital Equipment Corporation) in the early 1970s that allows computers to be connected and data to be sent at ten Mbps on a standard Ethernet.

E*Trade

A company founded by Bill Porter in 1982 to provide online information services to companies such as Fidelity, Charles Schwab and Quick & Reilly.
Porter wondered why he had to pay hundreds of dollars for stock exchange transactions, and thought that some day buyers would be able to buy and sell stock from their own computers.
The first use of E*Trade's online transaction technology was in 1983 by a doctor in Michigan. Years later, in 1992, E*TRADE Securities, Inc. was created and started providing online investment services through America Online and CompuServe.
In 1992, www.etrade.com was launched, and the demand for its services grew fast. In 1996, Porter passed the mantle of company director to Christos Cotsakos, who had more than 20 years' experience in business management and had been decorated in the Vietnam war with the purple heart and the bronze medal for his courage. Cotsakos has made use of his experience, making E*TRADE a significant player in the Internet world. Its website is at www.etrade.com

Eudora

One of the most popular e-mail programmes, developed by Steve Dorner in 1988 in the University of Illinois. Qualcomm bought the rights in 1991 and allows its free use. At present, *Microsoft* and *Netscape's* successful programs have reduced its number of users. Its website is at www.eudora.com

European Academic and Research Network

See EARN

Euroseek

A European *portal* and *search engine* established in Sweden in 1996. Its contents may be viewed in more than 39 different

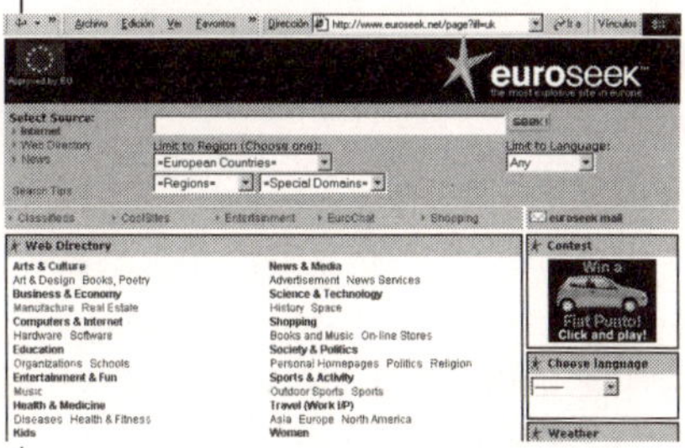

languages, which allows users from all European countries and from other continents to conveniently locate the information. By mid-2000, the search engine's database had stored 1.5 million websites and was receiving 30 million visits each month. Its website is at www.euroseek.com

Excite

One of the best *search engines* on the Internet, converted to a *portal* and the owner of *@Home*. It can be found at www.excite.com

See @HOME, @WORK

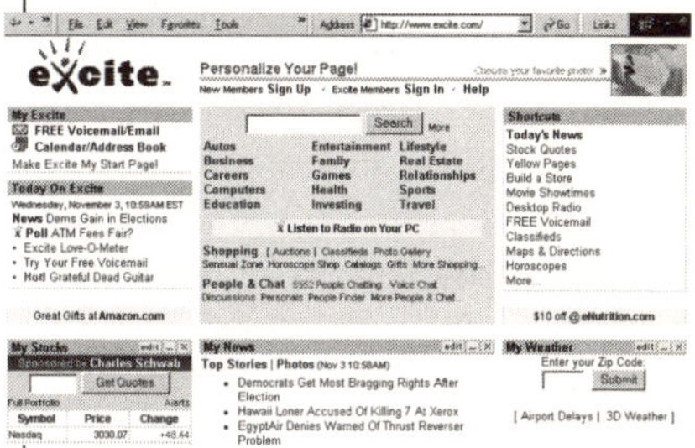

expansion program

Software used to expand files that have been compressed.

Explorer, Internet Explorer

One of the most popular *browsers* on the Internet, developed by *Microsoft* (the other is by *Netscape*). At present, it is provided free with Microsoft's Windows software due to the *browser war* that developed because of the major software companies manoeuvring to obtain the greatest market share. It can also be downloaded free online from www.microsoft.com.

Extensible Markup Language

See XML

extranet

An *Intranet* extended to the Internet, with the aim of allowing access to people and companies external to the organisation (providers, distributors, clients, etc.) in an authorised manner.

facilitated chat
A *chat* in which someone controls messages appearing on-screen and acts as *moderator*. Often used when there is a guest who is not to be overwhelmed by questions that cannot be answered during the chat or when there are heated debates.

FAQ (Frequently Asked Questions)
A list of questions most frequently asked by users on a specific subject. The answer can be found next to each question. They often refer to technical issues, software use, etc.
The Internet has a great many pages dedicated to these questions. They can be located via any portal by typing 'faq' in the search box; this will turn up FAQs on all imaginable subjects. Many websites include an FAQ area to solve user problems or any queries on content.
On many *LISTSERV* and *newsgroup* sites, FAQs cover the most common queries on the subject being discussed, so referring to them can save a lot of time.

favourite
See BOOKMARK

FCC (Federal Communications Commission)

FCC

A United States government independent agency, set up in 1934, responsible for regulating interstate and international communication by radio, television, telephone and cable. Its website is at www.fcc.gov

FDDI (Fibre Distributed Data Interface)
A high-speed *LAN* token *ring* which can transmit up to 100 Mbps. It uses fibre-optic cable.

Federal Communications Commission
See FCC

Fibre Distributed Data Interface
See FDDI

fibre-optic cable
See OPTICAL FIBRE

Fidonet
An amateur personal computer network which appeared in 1984, spread all around the world and in which thousands of *BBSs (bulletin board services)* participated. It allowed file sharing and e-mail, as well as participation in group *chats* via telephone connections. It has now practically disappeared.

file compression
See COMPRESSION

file server
A computer which provides files for remote users via a network.

file transfer
The process of transmitting files from one computer to another by means of a computer network.

File Transfer Protocol
See FTP

file types
Files can be stored in several different formats, depending on their contents: audio, text, video, images, etc. Some of the most frequent on Internet are:

GIF	for photographs and images
JPEG	for photographs
MPEG	for sound, video and animation
AVI	for video and animation
WAV	for sound
EXE	for executable programs
TIFF	for images

filter
Hardware or software which allows access to some Internet areas to be limited. Filters can be of different types, such as filters for content and e-mail filters. For example, a filter for adult content can be installed on *browser* to prevent children from accessing inappropriate websites. (There are filters for other contents.) An e-mail filter prevents unsolicited mail (*spam*) from arriving, or blocks unwanted mail from specified users.
See SurfWatch

Finger
Software which enables a user to know if a specific person is connected to Internet at any moment. This can be displayed as the user's real name, the terminal being used, or the hour and day that user last connected.
It was originally a UNIX command, and it is currently offered by several programes, such as *Netscape* Navigator. For security and privacy reasons, not all servers support Finger.

firewall
A security system on a local network or the Internet. It may be security hardware or software, or a combination of both. Generally, firewalls are placed between the Internet and a web server so as to prevent unauthorised access which could destroy, alter or obtain information from the local system.

First Tuesday
A meeting for Internet businesses, where people and companies offering capital, talent, technology, resources and expansion can contact each other. To identify different people according to their interests, start-up entrepreneurs wear green identification, investors wear red, and press and professional service providers wear yellow.
Meetings are held at fashionable places or convention centres, usually in the evening, and include presentations by new businesspeople and sponsors. There are currently First Tuesdays in a large number of cities round the world (over 60), and users can subscribe via the website. They also offer free mailing-list service, where subscribers can keep in touch on various subjects and receive invitations to events, as well as a work forum with job offers. The name comes from the first day the

event was held, the first Tuesday in October 1998 in London. The website is at www.firsttuesday.com.

flame
An insulting or angry message or complaint on a mail list or *newsgroup*. Flames usually appear when *Netiquette* rules are broken. If the person to whom a flame is sent answers with another, there is usually a *flame war*, where multiple flames are exchanged. The associated verb is 'flaming' and it is unfortunately a fairly frequent event.
See NETIQUETTE

flame mail
A *flame* sent by e-mail.

flame war, flame bait
A series of insulting messages (*flames*) placed in a discussion forum. Some users place messages of this sort to provoke flame wars. The result is an endless succession of e-mails and an increasing number of users involved in feeding the flame war.

flamer
A person who sends *flames*.

Flash

macromedia®
FLASH PLAYER

A software product, property of Macromedia, which allows creation of high-quality vector animation, and has the added advantage of using very little space and is thus quickly downloadable from the Internet. It also allows interactivity, and the user can execute specific orders via the menus.
Usually used for cartoons, maps, banners, etc. Documents created in Flash are usually stored in a format with the extension '.swf'.
Practically all current browers support it, although problems might be encountered with older versions. It is included in Windows 98, *Netscape* Navigator, *America Online* and the Apple Macintosh operating system. For browers which do not incorporate it, Flash Player can be downloaded free.
The example above shows Coca Cola's home page (www.cocacola.com), which uses this technology. See also www.macromedia.com.

Flash player
Software for viewing the contents of a *Flash* document.

flat rate
A fixed monthly fee for connection to the Internet charged by telecommunications

companies. It allows limitless *surfing* for a fixed tariff.

follow-up
An answer placed in a *newsgroup* which continues the conversation on the subject under discussion.

form
See E-FORM

forum
From the Latin 'forum', meaning the square in Rome where public business was discussed and where judgement was carried out.
See NEWSGROUPS

forward, forwarding
1 Sending an e-mail on to a third person is known as 'forwarding'.
2 The button on a browser toolbar which allows the user to advance through the sequence of visited websites.
See BACK BUTTON

frames
Divisions on a web page which make up two or more independent *HTML* sections, each of which is known as a frame and which can act separately. Some websites offer the possibility of surfing with or without frames, as some browsers (especially very old versions) do not allow the use of frames.
A typical use of frames is to have an index of the site on the left of the screen which, when clicked, changes the pages ing the right-hand area. The advantages are that the index is always visible and download time is reduced.

freemail
A service offering free e-mail in exchange for the user looking at advertisements or providing specific personal data. Its use has become quite frequent in *portals* and other information environments. The advantage is not having to pay for using it, and being able to access it from any computer connected to Internet simply by keying in a name and password. One of the best-known services is *Hotmail*, property of *Microsoft*.

freenet
A non-profit-making service which was quite successful in the USA, especially among domestic users. It consisted of free or reduced-price access to the Internet, generally for an hour a day, and was offered to users from a specific area or through public libraries. Those offering it are affiliated to the NPTN (National Public Telecomputing Network).

freeware
Free software that can be downloaded, copied and distributed from the Internet, such as some *plug-ins* and games. The downside is that, being free, there are not usually any upgrades or support. Freeware and *shareware* are different concepts; shareware can generally be used free for a limited time (usually 30 days) but

must then be paid for to continue using it (although not very large sums).
See SHAREWARE

Frequently Asked Questions
See FAQ

from:
Part of the *e-mail message* which specifies the person or company sending it.

FrontPage
A web-page design and creation program of the WYSIWYG (what-you-see-is-what-you-get) type, developed by *Microsoft*. It is one of the most widely used.

FTP (File Transfer Protocol)
One of the first standard Internet tools, widely known and used for its ease and speed. It is a protocol which allows files to be transferred, copied, moved and erased files from one computer to another (usually from a personal computer to a remote server and viceversa); this is independent of the kind of computer used and its location.
There are thousands of FTP servers from which public-use files (documents and programes) of all sorts can be downloaded. There are also *anonymous FTPs* where no password is required and the user's identity remains unknown.
When web pages are created or updated, FTP is used to transfer files from a personal computer to the server from which they will be offered to other Internet users. For this, a user ID and a password are required.
Other well-known standards are *HTTP (Hypertext Transfer Protocol)*, which transfers web pages and related documents, and *SMTP (Simple Mail Transfer Protocol)*, which transfers *e-mail*.

FTP Client
Software used to carry out *FTP*. It allows access between a personal computer and the FTP server.

FTP privileges
The privileges given by an *ISP* so that a user can carry out *FTP* from his/her personal computer directly to the server. Among these privileges is the password.

FYI (For Your Information)
An acronym often used in *e-mail messages*. Very typical as a heading on a mail document or copy sent to another person.

gateway
A computer which connects two or more networks or computers using different protocols and applications (i.e. which are incompatible) and allows them to communicate. It modifies data, that is, it converts protocols, allowing them to arrive at the receiving computer legibly.
Although similar in some respects, *Routers* are not to be mistaken for gateways.

GB (Gigabyte)
1 GB (Gigabyte) = 1,000 Megabytes.
1 GBps = 1 Gigabyte per second
See BIT, BYTE

Gb (Gigabit)
See BIT, BYTE

GBps
Gigabyte per second.
See BIT, BYTE

Gbps
Gigabit per second.
See BIT, BYTE

Geographic Information System
See GIS

GIF (Graphics Interchange Format)
A graphic format developed in the 1980s, identified by the file extension '.gif'. This is the most widely used method on the Internet for compressing and showing images (drawings and photographs) with up to 256 colours (eight bits) and sending them quickly over the Internet. There are two versions: GIF87a (defined in 1987) and *GIF89a* (defined in 1989) which allows the creation of images simulating animation as a short sequence, very often used in creation of advertising banners, usually called animated GIF. Linked versions show the image gradually while it is being downloaded, and GIF also allows the creation of transparent backgrounds. With these characteristics, GIF is used for buttons, backgrounds, frames, drawings, photographs and ads, etc. in web pages.
The other most frequently used format is *JPEG,* which is not limited to 256 colours, which makes it more appropriate for maintaining photo quality.

GIF89a
A version of the *GIF* format defined in July 1989. In comparison with the previous version (87a), the main advantage is that it allows the creation of animated images based on a short sequence of constantly repeating images. A typical example is an advertising banner.

Gigabit
See Gb

Gigabyte
See GB

GIS (Geographic Information System)
A system of geographical information which captures, analyses, handles and shows

results on data referring to world geography and customises them.
On the Internet, it is used in many ways: country and city plans (post codes, establishments, streets, etc.), meteorological information, roadmaps, population data, etc. The website is at www.gis.com

GMT (Greenwich Mean Time)
The time at the Greenwich Meridian, used as the standard on the Internet to have a time reference which is the same for all countries.
GMT references can be seen in many places on the Internet, e.g. on *chats* beginning at a specific time, meteorological information, news, etc.

Go Network
A portal belonging to the Walt Disney Internet Group and created jointly with *Infoseek*. It is oriented towards children and families and has a specialised *search engine*.
It can be found at www.go.com

Gopher
A system founded on a hierarchical text-based menu which organises and allows file and program searches on the Internet by common subject. Each menu contains links to files, to other Gopher sites or database *search engines*. This tool eases access to *FTP* server files, as well as *Telnet* and *Archie* files. Through Gopher, users can Telnet with remote computers and search databases. Each Gopher server has its own file and program menu. Access to these servers is via Gopher client software and some browsers.
Gopher was developed in 1991 by the University of Minnesota, and was named after their mascot (inhabitants of Minnesota are known as 'gophers').
It was very popular for years, especially with universities.
Gopher was a forebear of the *WWW*, but when *hypertext* links and graphic browsers (mainly *Mosaic*) appeared, Gopher fell into disuse, although it can still be accessed by means of browsers.
The most popular search tools are *Veronica* and *Jughead*.

Gopherspace
The space where all *Gopher* servers are found on the Internet. For users of the service, all these servers appear as a single unit. It is derived from the words 'Gopher' and '*Cyberspace*'.

GoTo

A company created in 1997 and based in California which offers a powerful search engine to facilitate searches, and which has lately extended business to other Internet areas. Its website is at www.goto.com

.gov
The domain-name suffix corresponding to a non-military American federal agency. It is reserved for exclusive US Government

use. Examples are: www.whitehouse.gov, www.dnfsb.gov and www.nasa.gov.
See DOMAIN

graphic
An image, drawing, photograph, etc. which appears on a web page, generally in non-text areas. The most-used formats are *GIF* and *JPEG*.

graphic image
See GRAPHIC

Graphical User Interface
See GUI

Greenwich Mean Time
See GMT

groupware
A term which describes the type of software allowing group work among different people, data-sharing and document make-up. The best known are Lotus Notes and Microsoft Exchange.

GUI (Graphical User Interface)
A graphic interface for users which presents icons and active areas instead of text and commands. The best-known examples are the operating systems of Apple Macintosh and Microsoft Windows.

guru
An expert renowned in a specific subject due to extensive knowledge; thus, electronic commerce gurus, security gurus, etc.

hacker

A person who can break a computer system's security and access the data on it. Hackers are usually very skilled programers who know the functioning of security systems very well.

If they act with malice, they are known as *crackers*. The two terms are often confused, and hackers are often blamed for malicious access to systems. If asked, a hacker will define him/herself as a computer expert. Those in charge of system security would probably say that hackers are malicious people who want to crash their systems, destroy data, cause diverse damage, leave aggressive or insulting messages, or carry out destructive or illegal actions.

In general, there are no clear definitions of hackers, nor are there limits to their actions. More information can be found on www.antionline.com.

HDML (Handheld Device Markup Language)

A programing language which predated *WML (Wireless Markup Language)* and which is already obsolete. It was used for showing documents created in *HTML* on mobile telephones and *PDAs (Personal Digital Assistant)* with small screens.

See WML

header

1 In an e-mail, the area before the message text with the sender's name, date and time.

2 In a data packet, the part before the data, containing the receiver's address, error verification systems, etc.

helper application

An external program added to a browser and used to open files not recognised by the browser. Usually used for images, audio and video.

history list

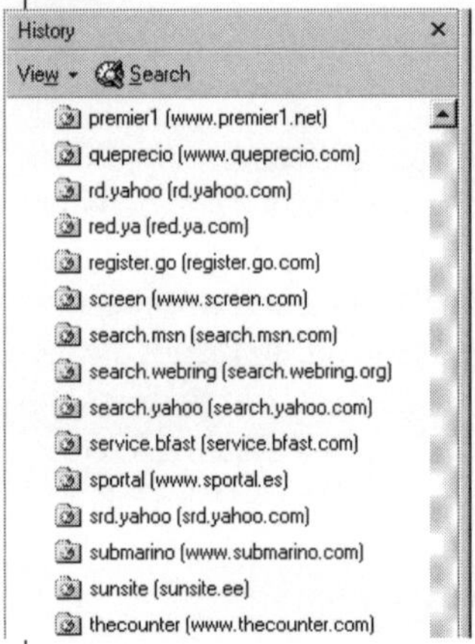

Some browsers keep a file of sites previously visited; it displays the names of sites that have been visited on certain days or during the preceding week. Users can return to listed pages by simply clicking on the link. The history list can be from the browser's menu bar or via an icon (see previous page).

hit
Each time a page is requested from an Internet server, it is considered a hit, and a record is kept on the server. This can go beyond the page itself to include images, audio, video, frames, etc. which can all register as different hits. If a page with text and three graphics is downloaded, it will count as four hits. It is not a reliable record of the number of visitors to a site, but it gives a general idea of the traffic.
The information on the number of hits on a website or a page is given by the page analysis software, and this can be used to check which pages are the most requested.

hit counter
See COUNTER

hoax
A joke sent by a malicious person, which spreads rapidly over the Internet, generally by e-mail. Hoaxes usually alarm people by announcing new viruses, and well-meaning users spread them to advise friends and acquaintances of the perils of the virus. This can cause company mail systems to crash.

home
See HOME PAGE

home button
The browser button which takes the user straight back to the page selected as the *home page*.

home page, homepage
1 The first page of a website, which acts as introduction, index and starting point for the rest of the site.
2 The first page that appears when the browser is opened. There is usually a default page defined by the company (e.g. *Netscape, Microsoft*) or the *ISP*, but this can usually be changed in the browser's preferences.

host
The *ISP* providing the Internet connection, and any server equipment on a network (and on the Internet) which provides services (sending files and information or storing websites) to other computers or users.

(web) hosting
Some *ISPs* provide space on their servers for their clients to place their web pages, thus allowing them to be accessed by other Internet users. Large companies usually store pages on their own computers, but web hosting is a good solution for people and small businesses who do then not need to maintain servers and permanent connections to the Internet.

HotBot
One of the largest search engines. It can be found at www.hotbot.com

hotlink
See LINK

hotlist
See BOOKMARK

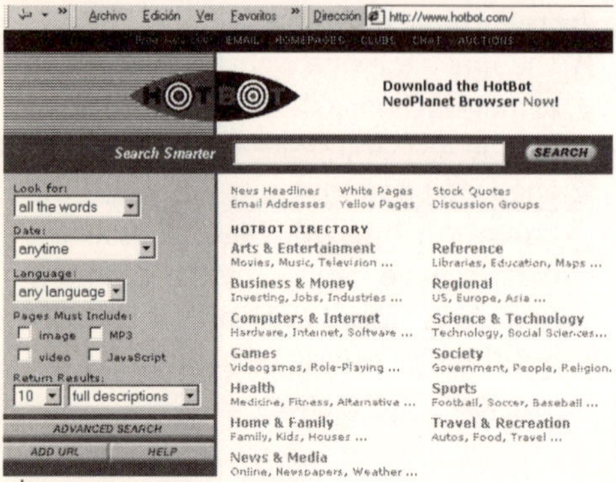

Hotmail

msn Hotmail®

A company acquired by Microsoft which used to provide a free e-mail service on the Web. It was a pioneer and had a great number of users.

hotspot

The area of an image on a web page which contains a link to another page.

htm

The same as *HTML*. With older operating systems (Windows 3.1 and OS 2), there was a limit to the number of characters which a file name could contain (eight characters for the name, and three for the suffix). For this reason, the suffix was '.htm' instead of 'html'. With current operating systems (mainly the new versions of Windows), this problem has disappeared and files ending '.html' are permissable.

HTML (Hypertext Markup Language)

This is not a programing language, but a system used to create and format hypertext documents on the World Wide Web, based on the *SGML* standard. HTML uses format commands called 'tags', spread throughout the document, which the browser recognises and uses to show *ASCII* text (colour, type size, underlining, etc.), images, links, etc. accurately. For example, <title>BMW</title> indicates that the word 'BMW' is a document title. Almost all Internet pages are created in HTML, and files use the extension '.html' (or '*htm*' to a lesser degree).

Rules and changes for HTML are established by the *World Wide Web Consortium (W3C)* so as to standardise the language. However, browsers sometimes show information in different ways, and often a website's home page will display a message saying 'This site can be viewed better by using such-and-such company's browser'.

HTML 2.0

HTML developed by the IETF work group. It is the standard for the main characteristics of HTML.

HTML 3.2

The recommendation of *W3C* from early 1996 representing the agreement on HTML characteristics in 1996, adding characteristics such as tables, *applets*, super- and subscripts, as well as compatibility with *HTML 2.0*.

HTML 4.0

The recommendation of *W3C*, with a first version in December 1997 and a second in April 1998. It enhanced the characteristics of the previous version, with scripting, frames, absorbed objects and more. It also has characteristics which improve access for disabled people.

HTML 4.01
The review of version 4.0 carried out in December 1999 in which errors were corrected and some changes carried out. The next version issued by the W3C has been called *XHTML*.

HTML document
See HTML

HTML editor
A text editor used for creating web pages in HTML format. One of the best known *FrontPage* by Microsoft.

HTTP (HyperText Transfer Protocol)
A protocol in use since 1990 which controls communication between a server and a customer of the World Wide Web, and document transfers on the Internet. Most Internet addresses begin with 'http: //'Each web server contains an HTTP *daemon* (HTTPD), a program which receives HTTP requests and manages them. From a browser (customer HTTP), users can request a *URL* address or click on a link on a web page. This request travels to the HTTP daemon of the destination server, which returns requested information.

HTTP 1.1
The version which offers pages quickest on browsers; developed by the *Internet Engineering Task Force (IETF)*.

HTTPD (HyperText Transfer Protocol Daemon)
Acts on requests coming from the rest of the Web so as to carry out the process needed for sending answers. Each web server includes an HTTPD.
See *daemon*.

HTTPS (Secure Hypertext Transfer Protocol)

An HTTP variant developed by *Netscape* to support safe transactions. It connects HTTP servers using *SSL*, coding and decoding user page requests and pages received from the web server.
When using the Netscape browser, a key or a closed-lock symbol appears in the bottom-left corner.
In Microsoft Internet *Explorer*, it appears on the right.

hyperlink
See LINK

hypermedia
Images, graphics, audio and video which contain a link which opens another document when it is clicked on.
See LINK

hypertext
Text (words or phrases) containing a link connecting one document to another. It generally appears in a different colour

from the rest of the document and is underlined. The cursor usually changes when it is placed over the text to indicate the existence of hypertext.
See LINK

Hypertext Markup Language
See HTML

Hypertext Transfer Protocol
See HTTP

IAB (Internet Advertising Bureau)

A non-profit-making organisation for improving the use and effectiveness of advertising on the Internet. Their website is at www.iab.net

IAB (Internet Architecture Board)

A technical consulting group belonging to the Internet Society.
Amongst other things, the IAB supervises the architecture of protocols and proceedings used on Internet and gives parameters for the processes used for creating standards. It is a support entity for the *IETF (Internet Engineering Task Force)*.
It was originally called the Internet Activities Board and was founded in 1983 with Dave Clark as its president. This was during the times when Internet was mainly an investigative tool for the US government. The IABs website is at www.iab.org

IANA (Internet Assigned Numbers Authority)

An authority originally responsible for distributing *IP addresses*, co-ordinating parameter assignments in protocols for technical standards on the Internet and controlling *DNS*, including the delegation of high-level domains.
Currently under the umbrella of *ICANN (Internet Corporation for Assigned Names and Numbers)*, IANA continues to distribute addresses to people registered on the Internet, co-ordinates, with the *IETF* and others, the assignment of protocol parameters, and supervises the operation of the DNS.
IANA is housed at the Information Sciences Institute, University of Southern California. Their website is at www.iana.org

ICANN (Internet Corporation for Assigned Names & Numbers)

A private, non-profit-making entity for technical co-ordination of the Internet. It was created in October 1998 by a group of technical, business, academic and user communities, and it has the responsibility for technical function areas previously dependant on the US government through *IANA* and other organisations. ICANN is responsible, amongst other things, for *domain* names on the Internet and *IP numerical addresses*. Its website can be found at www.icann.org

ICMP (Internet Control Message Protocol)
The standard protocol for generating error messages, packet control and information messages related to Internet protocol (IP), message errors and control on Internet systems.

icon

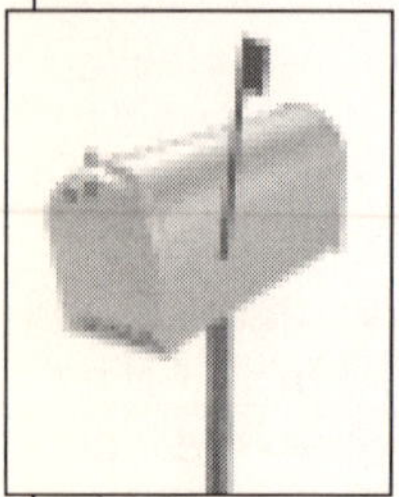

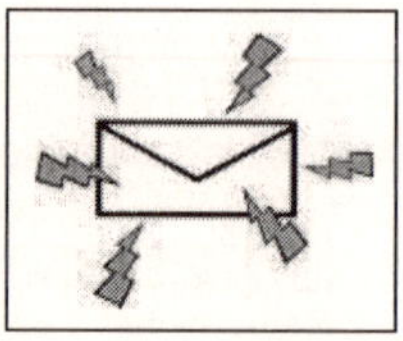

A Greek word meaning 'image'. In computing, it is a small image or drawing which graphically represents an object on a computer screen or web page. It is a basic component of a *GUI (Graphical User Interface)*. For example, a drawing of an envelope or a mail box on a web page means that clicking on it will send an e-mail.

ICQ ('I Seek You')
An Internet program that can be downloaded which allows users to find out who is connected to Internet and to initiate contact with them by sending messages, playing computer games or having *chats*. When downloading, a *user-ID* number is received to facilitate the registration process.

ICSA
A company, established in 1989, which is the leader in security control services for companies connected to the Internet. Its services reduce the risks and improve the quality of security set-ups on the Internet. It currently certifies almost 100% of antivirus software on the market, web firewalls, and products for the detection of intruders and coding. Its website is at www.icsa.net

IESG (Internet Engineering Steering Group)
Responsible for the technical management of *IETF* activities and standard processes on the Internet. It is a member of *ISOC (Internet Society)*, and administers processes according to ratified rules and proceedings.
It is responsible for the final approval of standard Internet specifications.

IETF (Internet Engineering Task Force)

An open, international community with many members which unites web designers, operators, commercial businesses and investigators in a group whose aim is to develop Internet architecture. Technical work is carried out by groups organised in areas of knowledge such as security, transport, routing, etc. The group was formally set up in 1986 under the presidency of Phil Gross. Its website can be found a www.ietf.org.

image map
See CLICKABLE IMAGE MAP

IMAP (Internet Mail Access Protocol)
A mail protocol which allows handling of e-mail. Users can review message subjects, create or delete mail files and messages, all without having to download mail onto their computer, as it is kept on the server.
The other well-known protocol is called *POP3 (Post Office Protocol 3)*. With this, when mail is accessed, it is downloaded onto the personal computer, deleting it from the server.
Neither protocol is to be mistaken for *SMTP*, a transfer protocol for e-mail between two Internet sites. It is necessary to have either IMAP or POP3 for reading e-mail after it has been received.

impression
A general term for each download and view of a web page from a server (page views). It is a more precise term than *hits*, as the latter counts the components of a page independently (for example, three images count as three hits). The number of impressions gives an indication of website success and is measured by means of special programs which analyse server information.
In advertising terms, it refers to how many times a banner is shown, measured in days or months. 'Impression' can be a synonym for 'ad view'.

inbound link
A link which draws traffic to a specific page from other areas on the Internet.

inbox

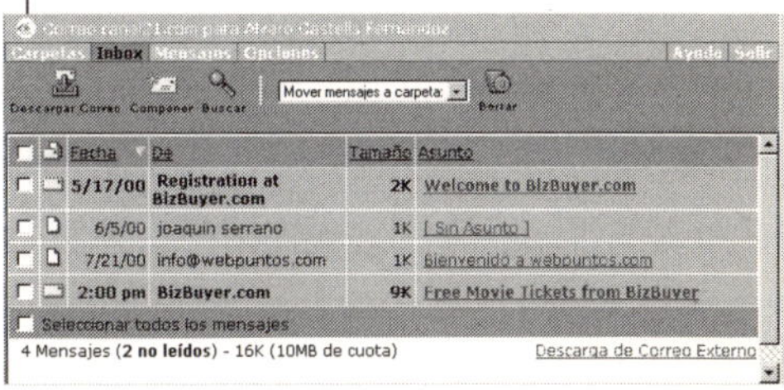

The file where e-mail is received. The example shows an inbox from free e-mail (www.canal21.com) displaying the messages that have come in, their headings, their size, and the person who sent them.

incubator
From the Latin 'incubare' meaning 'to hatch'. A name for a company which specialises in funding, developing and launching diverse Internet projects; the word is used because of the parallels between this business activity and the incubation of eggs to help the chicks hatch.

Infind
A metasearch engine. Find it at www.infind.com

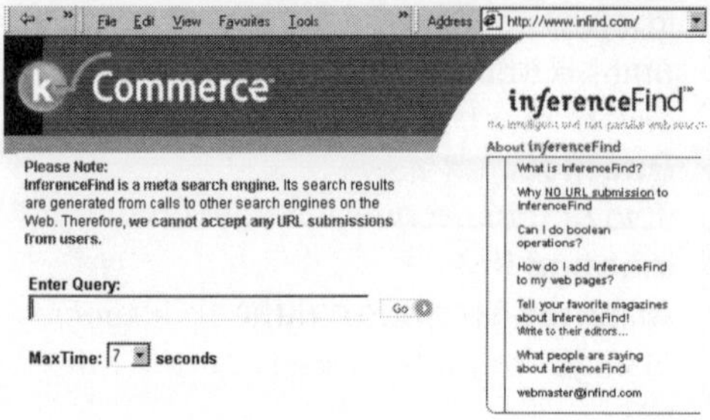

Infobahn
The German variation on *information superhighway*.

infobot
See MAILBOT

Infomedia
An Internet company which finds, stores and organises the information it offers its users. This word is also used for companies trading in electronic information. For example, infomediators on *B2B* carry out auctions, putting buyers and sellers in contact for a percentage share in the sale.

information packet
A set of data sent by a network.

information superhighway
An idealistic view of the Internet using a term popularised by Al Gore (then US Vice-President) who laid out the future of communications networks as a single, integrated, high-speed unit (Internet, cable television, telephone, leisure, etc.).

information technology
See IT

Infoseek

One of the best-known and most powerful search engines on the Internet. Currently integrated on www.go.com. (Its former address was www.infoseek.com)

Inktomi
An American company set up in 1996, a leader in Internet technologies, especially those related to search services and directories and services used by main *portals* and search engines. Its website can be found at www.inktomi.com

interlaced GIF
A characteristic of the *GIF* format which allows an image to develop gradually whilst being downloaded. At the beginning, the image is hardly recognisable, as it seems out of focus; however, it develops in successive layers until it is completely downloaded.

International Organisation for Standardisation
See ISO

International Telecommunication Union
See ITU

internaut
A person who surfs on the Internet.

Internet, the Net
A network begun in 1969 and made up of millions of computers connected to each other all over the world, using the standard *TCP/IP (Transmission Control Protocol/Internet Protocol)*. It is made up of the *World Wide Web*, *e-mail*, *FTP (file transfer protocol)*, *Gopher*, *USENET* newsgroups (discussion groups), *Telnet*, *IRC (Internet Relay Chat)* and other components. In the last few years, it has achieved a huge exponential growth in the number of users, servers and websites; this makes it one of the most relevant technologies in society today.
Its origins go back to the cold war between the USA and the Soviet Union, during which the US Defence Department created *ARPANet (Advanced Research Projects Agency)*, a web of military servers which could continue working even if one of them was destroyed. Later, in 1972, it spread out to the university and research fields, and in 1993, its commercial use was authorised.
The best-known areas on the Internet are e-mail and the World Wide Web, also known as WWW or the Web, and one of the characteristics which makes it most useful is the use of *hypertext*; this allows defined areas of text to take the user directly to other related pages when clicked. Besides hypertext, there are also links through images, drawings, audio and video which also take the user to other pages.
Through the WWW, millions of pages on every imaginable subject can be accessed. For this, *browsers* are used which allow the user to move through the pages, including image, audio and video. The best-known browsers are *Netscape* Navigator and Microsoft Internet *Explorer*.

internet
Two or more connected networks.

Internet Access Provider
See ISP

Internet account
An account set up with an *ISP (Internet Service Provider)* so as to have access to the Internet. Accounts can be paying or free.

Internet address
See ADDRESS

Internet Advertising Bureau
See IAB

Internet Architecture Board
See IAB

Internet Assigned Numbers Authority
See IANA

Internet Café
See CYBERCAFÉ

Internet Control Message Protocol
See ICMP

Internet Corporation for Assigned Names & Numbers
See ICANN

Internet Engineering Steering Group
See IESG

Internet Explorer
See EXPLORER

Internet Mail Access Protocol
See IMAP

Internet marketing
Traditional, real-world marketing methods which have been adapted to the Internet. In this new world, many concepts have changed, as traditional commerce has been substituted by *e-commerce*, mail and telephone have been substituted by *e-mail* and *chat*, traditional catalogues by website information and much more. This demands that professionals adapt and learn new rules.
There are countless websites which explain subjects related to marketing as well as listing specific associations.

Internet Network Information Centre
See INTERNIC

Internet Protocol (IP)
Used for connecting networks over the Internet. It is a transport protocol, used as the basis of the Internet, which directs the way information is sent from one area of the Web to another, in packets which re-assemble when they reach the other end. When a web page is received by a browser, the information arrives in small packets which reunite to create the page.

Internet Protocol Address
See IP ADDRESS

Internet Protocol Number
See IP NUMBER

Internet Protocol Version 6
See IPV6

Internet Relay Chat
See IRC

Internet Research Task Force
See IRTF

Internet Service Provider
See ISP

Internet server
See SERVER

Internet Society (ISOC)

A non-government, non-profit-making organisation founded in January 1992 and housed at Reston, Virginia. It is made up of international experts and gives support to the growth and development of the Internet, as well as co-ordinating standards, technology and applications.
By mid-2000, it was made up of over 150 organisations and 6,000 members in over 100 countries.
It is the leader in subjects related to the future of the Internet, and is the parent organisation of groups responsible for Internet infrastructure standards, including the *IETF (Internet Engineering Task Force)* and the *IAB (Internet Architecture Board)*. It manages global cooperation and co-ordination on the Inter-

net, as well as interconnection technology and its applications. Its website is at www.isoc.org

Internet World

Possibly the best-known Internet fair in the world. It is held four times a year in different US cities, and every year in several countries round the world. It gathers exhibitors related to all fields of knowledge and business on the Internet, and simultaneously holds conferences, forums and presentations of new technology. The website is at www.pentonevents.com where there is also information on other fairs.

Internet2

A non-profit-making organisation made up of over 170 US universities working in association with companies (usually related to telecommunications) and the government to develop and offer advanced web applications and technology, allowing the accelerated development of the Internet.

Internet2 re-forges existing links between universities, industry and government which gave place to the current Internet. Contrary to popular belief, Internet2 is not a separate physical network which will replace the current one, but rather it develops new technology and capacities which can be used on the Internet. As an example, their current projects include work on IPV6 and high bandwidth for multimedia applications.

They also work in collaboration with NGI (*Next Generation Internet*) in many areas. Their website is at www.internet2.edu

InterNIC (Internet Network Information Centre)

An organisation made up of the NSF (National Science Foundation), Network Solutions Inc. and AT&T. It is the centre responsible for several areas on the Internet, although it is better known for registering and maintaining *domain* names such as .com, .edu, .gov, .net and .org. If someone wants a domain name with one of these suffixes, they must check if it is registered and, if it is free, register it on InterNIC (or do so via another company which acts as intermediary and charges for the service).

Another kind of domain, the geographic one for countries, is administered by US Domain Name Registration Services and by the countries themselves.

InterNIC's website is at www.internic.net
See DOMAIN

intranet
A private network similar to the Internet, often using the same tools and software (browsers, etc.) and typical Internet protocols, such as *TCP/IP*, *HTML* and *HTTP*, but on a much smaller scale. Intranets are usually used by companies to increase efficiency and improve information channels and groupwork among employees. They frequently include connections to the Internet.

IP
See INTERNET PROTOCOL

IP address (Internet Protocol Address)
Identifies a specific computer address on the Internet with a unique number such as 199.26.226.7. The number is subdivided into four decimal numbers, each between 0 and 255, separated by dots, with each number representing eight bits (a 32-bit address). This number (also called a 'dotted quad') is unique, and without it, no Internet protocols could be used. This definition is based on the use of protocol for Internet version 4 (Internet Protocol Version 4); Version 6 describes new IP addresses with 128 bits, which will boost the number of increasingly scarce free IP addresses. To be part of the Internet, it is necessary to have this number, which is obtained on request from the *Network Information Centre* (NIC).
It can be compared to a telephone number. When a specific number is dialled, a connection is made to a specific telephone. When an IP number address is dialled, a connection is made to the computer which has this number assigned to it.
It can also be written as a text address (although sometimes containing numbers too). To translate numeric IP addresses to web address names, *domain* name servers are used.
An example of an IP address expressed in numeric mode is 207.37.253.203, which corresponds to www.atkearney.com.
See DNS

IP number (Internet Protocol Number)
The numeric version of an Internet address; it is made up of a unique number in four parts divided by dots, which identifies a specific computer on Internet, for example 197.222.12.56.
See IP ADDRESS, DNS

IPV6 (Internet Protocol Version 6)

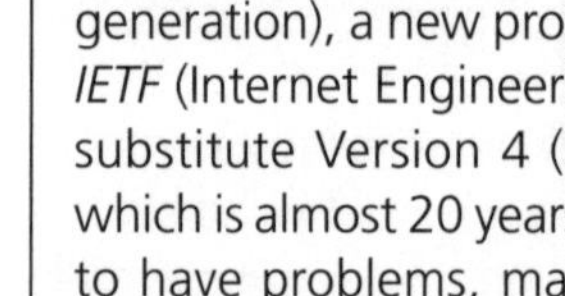

Also called IPng (Internet Protocol next generation), a new protocol designed by *IETF* (Internet Engineering Task Force) to substitute Version 4 (IPV4). Version 4, which is almost 20 years old, is beginning to have problems, mainly because it is running out of free addresses, but it is also outdated in terms of routing and web self-configuration. Version 6 will gradually substitute Version 4, but they will coexist for years.

Version 6 can be installed as a software upgrade on Internet devices and is compatible with IPV4, having been designed to work correctly on high-performance networks while still being adequate for low band-width networks. The website is at www.ipv6.com

IRC (Internet Relay Chat)
A pioneering *chat* programe which allows direct conversations to be held with users all over the world by writing messages that others can read and answer immediately. It is made up of several separate IRC server networks, which allow users to connect to IRC. The main ones are EFnet (the pioneer), Undernet, IRCnet, DALnet and NewNet.
In mid-1988, the Finn Jarkko Oikarinen presented irc1.0 and began to operate the first IRC server. Michael Sandrof launched ircll a year later, the first IRC customer.
In 1991, there were 500 users, and by the end of 1997 there were 175,000; currently, the number is enormous.
When a user connects to a server, his/her nickname (a fictitious name which replaces a person's real name, for example, 'superman') is registered as up to eight or 32 characters, depending on the network. IRC is made up of channels, or rooms, and each channel is preceded by the symbol +, & or #, the latter being the most frequent. This way, a sports channel will be called #sports.
On each channel, users can talk about a specific subject, with several people at the same time, or just one person, if they prefer to hold private conversations. There are usually people controlling conversations on the channels, known as channel operators or 'Ops'. When inadequate or insulting subjects come up, they can ban the user, and can also name new Ops and new IRC subjects. If a user does not agree with the Ops, he or she can create a new channel.
Each channel has topics about specific subjects on that channel. For example, 'Topic for sports: baseball players. Set by Trevor'; topics sum up the subject to be discussed.
IRC has its own terms which are useful to know:

IRC	Internet Relay Chat
Channel	chat room
Mode	adjusts channel or user
ChanOp	channel operator
IrcOp/Oper	IRC Server Operator
Kick	expel from a channel by an Op
Ban	permanent expulsion from a channel
Kiln/Glenn	outlawed on a server
LOL	Laughing Out Loud
ROFL	Rolling On the Floor Laughing
re's/rehi	hello again
wb	welcome back
brb	be right back
afk	away from keyboard

Besides channels in English, there are also other languages, such as #espanol (Spanish), #russian, #nippon (Japanese), #42 (Finnish), #warung (Malay) and #polska (Polish). Practically all languages are represented; if one isn't, a new channel can be created.
Related websites are www.irchelp.org and www.irc.net.
See ACRONYM, CHAT

IRTF (Internet Research Task Force)
A sub-group of the *IAB*, made up of Internet investigators who solve technological challenges which arise. The subjects they work on are related to protocols, applications, architecture and technology on the Internet.
Visit www.irtf.org.

ISDN (Integrated Services Digital Network)
A digital connection which allows a much higher speed than analogue connections, reaching 128,000 bps (bits per second) or 128 Kbps. It needs an ISDN terminal and a special modem. An ISDN line contains two channels of 64 Kbps each, which, when added together, make up 128 Kbps. It can be installed at home or in offices, and the same line can be used simultaneously for voice and data.

ISO (International Organisation for Standardisation)

ORGANISATION INTERNATIONALE DE NORMALISATION ISO INTERNATIONAL ORGANIZATION FOR STANDARDIZATION

An association responsible for setting up international standards in many areas, including information technology and telecommunications.
Visit www.iso.ch.

ISOC
See INTERNET SOCIETY

ISP (Internet Service Provider)
Also sometimes called an IAP (Internet Access Provider), a company or organisation which offers Internet access as well as other related services. ISPs generally charge a monthly or yearly sum for access, although there are many free-access services. They have a line permanently connected to the Internet, through which they accord access to their customers. Users usually gain access to the ISP server through a *modem* and telephone line; this server checks their ID by name and password, and allows them access to the Internet. ISPs offer additional services of all kinds, most commonly e-mail accounts, web-page hosting, etc.
In the USA, the most outstanding are MCI and AT&T. *America Online* offers an enormous number of services besides simple Internet connection, and has millions of users. These services are often called OSPs (online service providers).

IT (Information Technology)
An area taking in everything related to computing and technology.

ITU (International Telecommunication Union)
One of the first telecommuncations organisations. ITU's story is basically the story of world telecommunications. The milestones they have achieved are the basis for new telecommunications. On 24th May 1844, Samuel Morse sent the first public message by means of a telegraph wire between Washington and Baltimore. Ten years later, the telegraph was made public. However, at this time, telegraph wires did not cross borders between countries, as each country used a different system and their own telegraph code to

keep military and political messages confidential. Messages had to be transcribed, translated and re-sent to the neighbouring country's telegraphic web. At this point, the countries involved decided to reach agreements, and 20 European countries decided to meet to work on a general agreement, as well as standard rules for equipment and connection guarantees. After over two years' negotiations, in 1896 they signed the first International Telegraph Convention and set up the International Telegraph Union to continue work subsequent to the agreements they had reached. This was the birth of the ITU, and 130 years later, its foundation aims are still in effect.

It was later involved in telephone issues, wireless telegraphy, radio and space-radio communications. It is currently taking on subjects related to the new telecommunications webs, and the importance these have for development of the Internet. Its headquarters are in Geneva (Switzerland).

Its website is at www.itu.org

jargon
Language used by Internet experts. There is hacker jargon, cracker jargon, etc.

Java

A solid, object-oriented programing language launched in May 1995 by *Sun Microsystems* (John Gage) and *Netscape* (Marc Andreessen); similar to *C++*, Java was created in 1991 as a programing tool by Patrick Naughton, Mike Sheridan and James Gosling of Sun, and was intended to be incorporated into Netscape Navigator.
It is the valid standard for all types of platforms, such as Windows, Macintosh and *UNIX*. It is represented by a coffee cup, referring to the coffee from the Indonesian island. It can also be used to write short programes, given the name Java *applets*, which can be downloaded from a web server and run on a computer (client side) through a Java-compatible browser. These days, all of the major browsers are compatible.
Java applets are useful for extending the capabilities of an HTML page, and carrying out small functions in a computer such as animation, clocks, calculators, interactive games and animated text, as well as sound and video effects. Java has evolved a great deal, becoming a computer platform on which software developers can write all kinds of applications, such as word processing, accounting, human resource or stock-exchange programes. Although often confused because of the similarities between words, it is very different from *JavaScript*.
Visit the website at www.java.sun.com

Java applets, Java applications
Programs written in the *Java* programing language which can be included in an HTML page, and are run from a compatible browser (Java Virtual Machine). Most modern browsers support applets.

Java Database Connectivity
See JDBC

JavaBean
JavaBeans, otherwise known as Java coffee beans, also use the coffee symbol used by Sun for its *Java* programing language. These are developed using the 'Beans Development Kit' (BDK) from Sun, and are suitable for multiple platforms (Windows 95, UNIX, Mac) within many applications called 'containers', such as browsers, word processors, etc.
JavaBeans are small, reusable software objects (components) created in Java, which can be combined with other components in the same computer or in other compu-

ters in a network to create an application. They make it possible to incorporate interactive capabilities into web pages. For example, they are used to vary the contents of the pages depending on the type of user.

JavaScript
A programing language developed by *Netscape* for developing functions on the Internet client side. More complex than the *HTML* tags, it is embedded into the HTML page and is recognised by the browser. Its main function is to assemble interactive web sites. In spite of the similarity in name, it has nothing to do with *Java*. Its website is www.jsworld.com.

JavaScript Beans
Pieces of JavaScript code stored in a file with other information.

JDBC (Java DataBase Connectivity).
Enables a Java *applet* to contact a database and get information or update data.

Jini

Architecture technology, developed by *Sun Microsystems*, based on the simple concept that all devices can work together just by being connected. In this way, drivers, cables and connectors are eliminated. Devices are immediately available and start working just by being connected. In this way, you can connect your *PDA* to a computer and a mobile phone simultaneously without having to upload any software or make complicated connections. Visit the website at www.jini.org

JPEG (Joint Photographic Experts Group)
An image compression format developed by the Joint Photographic Experts Group, which is frequently used on the Internet and optimised for storing millions of different colours. It gives better image compression with more different colours than the *GIF* format. Compression can be done on several levels; the higher the compression, the less space taken up by the file, but there is also a greater loss in quality. The compressed images are identified by the file extension '.jpg' or '.jpeg'.

Jughead (Jonzy's Universal Gopher Hierarchy Excavation And Display)
A program for carrying out searches in *Gopher* server directories. Similar to *Veronica* and *Archie*.

junk e-mail
See SPAM

Kb (Kilobit, Kbits)
1 Kb (Kilobit) = 1,024 bits
1 Kbps (Kilobit per second) = 1,000 bits per second
See BIT, BYTE, KB

KB (Kilobyte)
1 KB (Kilobyte) = 1,000 bytes
1 KBps (Kilobyte per second) = 1,000 bytes per second
See BIT, BYTE, Kb

Kbps (Kilobits per second)
A unit used to measure modem speed, and the maximum number of bits that can be transferred per second in optimum conditions.
See BIT, BYTE, Kb

Kbps (Kilobytes per second)
A byte is eight bits; another measure of data-transfer speed.
See BIT, BYTE, KB

Kermit
A file-transfer protocol developed by Columbia University that works on the majority of operating systems. Mainly used in universities, files can be downloaded from remote servers onto a computer.

keyword
A word used in searches to locate websites or web pages.

killer app
A computer application that is very advanced and becomes very popular, eclipsing its competitors.

Kilobit
See Kb

Kilobits per second
See Kbps

Kilobyte
See KB

Kilobytes per second
See KBps

knowbie
Someone who knows a lot about the Internet and its functioning base. Opposite of a *newbie*.

LAN (Local Area Network)
A network that communicates between computers in a limited area, e.g. within a building or on the same floor. Many LANs are connected to the Internet.

latency, delay
From the Latin 'latens'. The time taken in the trajectory of a data package from its source to its destination.

LDAP (Lightweight Directory Access Protocol)
The standard established by the *IETF (Internet Engineering Task Force)* for directory services.

leased line
A telephone line connected exclusively between a user or a network and another network or an *ISP (Internet Services Provider)*. This is used when high-speed transmission is required.

Lightweight Directory Access Protocol
See LDAP

link, hyperlink
The area of an *HTML* document (text or graphics) that, when clicked on, takes the user to another page or to a different area of the document. Links enable pages of a website or even different websites to be connected, making navigation easier.
Links can be identified in several ways:
- the text can be marked in another colour or underlined;
- the cursor can turn into a pointing hand when it is moved over a link;
- the cursor changes colour or shape when it passes over an image or graphics containing a link.

linking

The process of connecting Internet pages through *links*. This enables users to go from one specific page to another, which could be in a server on the other side of the world.

Linux
A free operating system based on UNIX, created by the Finn, Linus Torvalds (shown above) in 1991 and subsequently expanded by developers from all over the world working in collaboration. There is no official support, and assistance comes from users and developers. In a very short space of time, it has become one of the world's most popular operating systems. Its advantages are its stability and speed, and the fact that it is not a system with commercial aims, but one that offers free access and is free of charge. The code is open, and anybody can access it to change it.

It is available for almost all platforms: PC, PowerPC, Macintosh, Amiga, Atari, DEC Alpha, Sun and others. Its websites are www.linux.org and www.linux.com.

LISTSERV
A program used to manage e-mail lists for users interested in certain subjects. Users send and receive e-mail to and from other users. The software automatically signs users up and cancels their names from the list as well as letting them receive, eliminate and distribute e-mail. When the program receives an e-mail request from a new user, they are signed up immediately; the same thing happens to eliminate users who are no longer interested in receiving mail, or addresses that are no longer active.
See MAILING LIST, MAJORDOMO

live cam
See WEBCAM

load
Abbreviation of *download* or *upload*.

Local Area Network
See LAN

location
See ADDRESS

log file
A file storing all the events that take place in a computer system. On the Internet, analysis of the log provides detailed information of the user's habits, the most-visited pages, the area from which they come, the number of pages downloaded, etc.

login, logon
Access to a computer system, generally after entering a user ID and password.

logout, logoff
The process of ending access to a specific computer; disconnection.

Lucent Technologies

An American company of Bell Laboratories, recognised within the world telecommunications market. Its website is at www.lucent.com

lurk
To read the messages in mailing lists, *USENET* newsgroups or *chat rooms* without taking part in them. Generally, it refers to the attitude that is taken when someone goes into a chat room for the first few times, and is unfamiliar with the subjects being discussed.

lurker
A person who *lurks*, reads the discussion going on in *chat rooms*, *USENET* newsgroups and mailing lists, but does not make any comments.

lurking
The action derived from the verb 'to *lurk*'.

Lycos
A North American company set up in 1995, which possesses, among other sites,

Lycos.com (one of the main Internet search engines), Tripod (www.tripod.com), Angelfire, Whowhere (www.whowwhere.com), MailCity, HotBot, HotWired (www.wired.com), Wired News, Webmonkey, Suck.com, Quote.com (www.quote.com), Sonique and Gamesville.

Its original search engine and directory started out with a patent for intelligent spidering technology originally created at the University of Canegie Mellon. By mid-2000, it had 33 million visitors a month and 148 million pages visited daily. It has now been acquired by Terra, a *portal* of the Telefónica group.

Its website is at www.lycos.com

Lynx

A text-based Internet *browser* (it does not support graphics) distributed by the University of Kansas, which became very popular. However, its inability to handle graphics makes its use more limited. There are versions of Lynx for PC, Mac, *UNIX* and VMS. Its website is www. ukans.edu.

LZH

File compression format that can be used with the LHA program created by Haruyasu Yoshizaki.

LZW (Lempel-Zefv Welch)

A method of *compression*.

mail
See E-MAIL

mail bomb/bombing
The act of crashing an e-mail address by sending a large number of messages from one or more people. The messages sent are usually unpleasant or have very large files attached, which do not make sense to the person to whom they are being sent. They are sent to people or organisations who have annoyed the 'mail bombers' in some way. Typical victims are people who have sent massive amounts of unsolicited commercial mail (*spamming*).
By doing this, the mail servers usually collapse and this causes problems for the recipient of the mail bomb, as they are subsequently unable to receive their normal mail correctly.

mail filter
Software that stops specific incoming mail, such as *spam.*

mail reflector
A program that automatically distributes data or files to subscribers to a mailing list, *USENET* group or *IRC* channel.

mail server
See E-MAIL SERVER

mailbot
An e-mail server that automatically responds to requests for information by sending out a message.

mailbox
A directory storing e-mail messages that are sent to individuals. This directory can be located on a personal computer or on an *ISP* mail server.

mailing list
A list of e-mail addresses to and from which messages can be sent. This is usually a discussion group made up of people who have common interests and who all receive messages on a regular basis. By subscribing, a user can send messages to all other users on the list, and at the same time, every time a user sends mail, everyone on the list will receive it. Some lists are moderated, where the *moderator* approves the contents that are sent in the mail. There are thousands of subjects to subscribe to, generally by sending an e-mail to the indicated address.

Majordomo
From the Latin 'maior' and 'domus', the principal servant of the house who is responsible for its economic management. This is a program written in the *Perl* programing language which handles Internet mailing lists automatically. The commands are sent to Majordomo by e-mail to handle the maintenance aspects of the lists, and, as a result, it is not necessary to access the Majordomo server.

marketplace
A virtual market where companies buy and sell products of all types. These are divid-

ed into vertical and horizontal markets. The vertical markets offer products directly related to that sector, such as, for example, cement if it is a construction marketplace. The horizontal markets offer general products required by all types of companies, such as pens or travel agency services. For example, www.mro.com and www.bizbuyer.com are both horizontal *portals*; www.metalsite.com and www.verticalnet.com are vertical portals.

Matrix

A cyber-thriller written and directed by the Wachowski brothers in 1999, with Keanu Reeves and Laurence Fishburne playing the leading roles. The planet's inhabitants believe they live in a real world. But it is actually only a dream, a complicated plot created by an artificial intelligence computer program that dominates the characters' lives.
Along with *Blade Runner*, one of two cult films among the Internet community. The website is at www.whatisthematrix.com

MB
See MEGABYTE

Mb
See MEGABIT

MBONE (Multicast BackbONE)
A network for real time Internet audio-conferencing and video-conferencing applications. This enables the same files to be sent simultaneously to multiple users (multicast).

MBps
Megabytes per second.

Mbps
Megabits per second.

mega
A prefix indicating 'thousand', such as in *Megabit* or *Megabyte*.

Megabit, Mb
A million bits, or, to be more exact, 1,048, 576 bits. This is represented as 'Mb'. It is commonly used to indicate transfer ratio (Megabits per second (Mbps)).
1 Mbps = 1 Megabit per second = 1,000,000 bits per second.
See BIT, BYTE

Megabyte, MB
1 MB (Megabyte) = 1,000 Kilobytes;
1 MBps = 1 Megabyte per second.
See BIT, BYTE

meta-tag

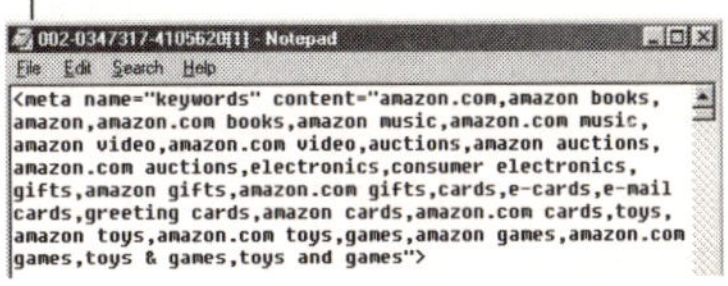

The HTML code placed at the beginning of the page in a 'tag' which contains information on the contents of a web page and of the website. Meta-tags are used to provide page information to *robots* and *search engines* that locate websites to be included in searches. As a result, page title, *keywords* and page descriptions are included. The keywords serve to help the search engine carry out the search for words, while the description included along with the *URL* address gives the user more information on the address being offered. When viewing the page through the browser, the meta-tag is only visible if the HTML code is opened. The example on the previous page shows the meta-tag for Amazon's *home page*.

Metacrawler

A well-known *metasearch* owned by Go2 Net (www.go2net.com), one of the most-visited Internet sites. It offers directory services, finances, multi-user games and other services. Its website is at www.metacrawler.com

metasearch
A search engine which employs multiple other search engines to trawl the Web simultaneously. When a search request is sent out, the metasearch sends this to more than one search engine or directory, responding with the addresses located in all of them.

micropayments
A system of making small payments on the Internet, mainly for intangible products. This system replaces credit-card payments, as the minimum commissions charged by the credit-card companies are too high to make this type of transaction worthwhile. For example, if a user were to search the 'house for sale' of a classified ads site using very specific characteristics, the results would be very limited; the charge for this service will be minimal on a pay-as-you-go system. Paying for this with a traditional credit card would cost more in commission charges than the actual cost of the service.

Microsoft
Anyone who is in any doubt about this company should visit www.microsoft.com.

.mil
A domain name extension, abbreviation of 'military'. It is one of the extensions that can be chosen when a domain check is requested. The websites that use this domain name usually correspond to North American military organisations, as the use of this domain is exclusive to the United States, for example: www.navy.mil, www.army.mil, www.darpa.mil.
See DOMAIN

MIME (Multipurpose Internet Mail Extensions)
A group of Internet extensions for *SMTP (Simple Mail Transfer Protocol)* which expand normal e-mail capacity, making it possible to attach electronic documents to the message, indicating to a computer

what type of program is required to open the file. When the files arrive with the mail in binary mode, MIME enables the documents to be recognised and 'translated'. In this way, images, videos, applications, word-processing documents and spreadsheets, etc. can be sent.
See BINHEX, UUENCODE

mirror, mirror sites

1 Where the same information is contained in two pieces of equipment, which can be physically separated or not. If one of these fails, the other would continue to offer information. This type of installation is used in Internet servers that have to be permanently connected to the Net, for example bank servers.
2 Some websites and *FTP* sites are so popular, and have so many access routes, that they have mirror servers in other areas or running in parallel so that they can offer higher quality and speed when accessing information. Placing mirrors in other areas has the advantage that access from the nearest area can be faster. For this reason, it is common for European websites that are visited a lot to have mirrors in the United States, where there is a lot more traffic. The mirror sites are continually updated to ensure that they contain the same information as the original website, and are normal in newspapers, *portals* and *search engines*.

.misc (misc newsgroup)

A higher category of the *USENET* newsgroups specialising in subjects that do not fit in other categories (miscellaneous). Other categories of newsgroups are .alt (alternative), .news, .comp (computer), .sci (science), .biz (business), .talk, .rec (recreational) and.soc (social). These newsgroups can be accessed via the majority of Internet browsers.
See NEWSGROUPS

MIT (Massachusetts Institute of Technology)

An educational institution founded in 1861, it has a prestigious reputation for its training and research in science and technology. It is made up of five academic colleges: the School of Architecture and Planning, the School of Engineering, the School of Humanities and Social Science, the Sloan School of Management and the School of Science. Its website is at www.mit.edu

mobile portals

Portals that have recently appeared for use with *PDA*-type mobile devices or mobile telephones. They offer the user information similar to that found on the Internet, but adapted to the screen, transmission speed and functions of these devices.

modem

From the words 'modulation-demodulation'. The modem is a piece of equipment (which can take the form of a box, card, etc.) that connects computers through standard or *ISDN* telephone lines, and transmits information converting the signal from analogue (telephone) to digital (computer) and vice versa. The conversion from digital to analogue is called modulation, and conversion from analogue to digital is called demodulation. The analogue signal can be transmitted by telephone lines. There are also cable modems. Modems can be internal (inside the computer) or external, with data transfer at different velocities, such as 300, 1200, 2400, 9600, 14400, 28800, 33600 and 56000 bits per second, the last two being the most frequently used at present.

modem cable
A modem unit that can be connected to a television or computer through the local cable connection, with the aim of accessing the Internet at a much higher speed than that of traditional modems.

modem pool
A group of modems that respond to the same telephone number and connect the caller with a specific resource. For example, *ISPs* have these modem groups to make accessing the Internet easier for their clients.

moderated mailing-list
A mailing list in which mail is sent to a *moderator* to check that the contents are appropriate before being sent on to its destination. If the moderator considers that the mail should not be sent, the mail is cancelled, and a message will be sent to the original sender explaining the reasons for the cancellation.

moderated newsgroup, discussion
A *newsgroup* that uses the presence of a *moderator* to categorise topics, organise messages and eliminate those that are unsuitable.

moderator
Someone who controls the information in e-mails, *USENET* newsgroups and *chats*, with the aim of preventing inappropriate, insulting or commercial messages from being sent.

Monster

monster.com

One of the best-known job-search websites, which puts companies looking for personnel into contact with people looking for work.
Monster.com is a company from Indianapolis belonging to the TMP Worldwide group, which resulted from the merger between The Monster Board and Online Career Center, founded in 1994 and 1993 respectively. Its website is at www.monster.com

MOO (MUD, Object-Oriented)
See MUD

Mosaic
A graphic Internet browser developed by the *NCSA (National Center for Supercomputing Applications)* at the University of Illinois. It was the first to appear and popularise the Internet before the advent of the current market leaders, *Netscape* Navigator and Microsoft Internet *Explorer.*

.mov
A video format whose extension comes from the word 'movie'.

Mozilla

The original name of Netscape Navigator before it became Netscape Communicator. It is an organisation made up of *Netscape* and independent computer developers, responsible for maintaining and improving the source code of the Netscape Communicator browser. Mozilla is based on a very early version of Netscape Communicator 5.0. Its website is at www.mozilla.org

MP3 (MPEG 3)
MPEG 1 layer 3 is the standard audio compression format, massively used on the Internet to distribute music. It enables the user to obtain high sound quality using high compression ratios. The first physical device to appear was the Diamond Rio, and on the Internet, you can find many software players, such as *Winamp*.

MP3.com

A company created in Delaware in March 1988, and one of the most visited in the Internet music environment. Its foundation lies in the development that has taken place in *MP3* music over the last few years, working with thousands of musicians and hundreds of independent labels to promote and sell their music. By mid-2000, it contained over half a million songs by 81,000 artists.
Surfers can search, listen to fragments and download the music free of charge. Its website is at www.mp3.com

MPEG, mpeg, mpg (Moving Pictures Expert Group)

One of the standards used on the Internet for audio and video files, as it allows the user to compress files, making transmission and downloading much faster. It uses the '.mpg' suffix. Other formats are *AVI* and *QuickTime*.
Its website is at www.mpeg.org

MPEG 3
See MP3

MSN (The Microsoft Network)

One of the most-visited *portals* in the world, owned by Microsoft. Among other services, it offers free e-mail via *Hotmail,* and local versions of the portal for different countries. Its address is www.msn.com.

MUD (Multi-User Dungeon or Multi-User Dimension)
An online adventure game similar to 'Dungeons and Dragons' that lets several play-

ers play simultaneously. These are role-play games in which the players take on the identities of fictional characters and follow instructions to complete the adventure. They are usually based on text mode and accessed via *Telnet*, or other client programes that can display 3D graphics, and *chat rooms*.

Multicast
Technology for real-time 'one-to-many' and 'many-to-many' communication through a network. The information is sent out simultaneously from a source point to many destinations.

multimedia
The interactive combination of text, animation, graphics, audio and video material.

Multipurpose Internet Mail Extensions
See MIME

Multi-User Dungeon
See MUD

NAK (Negative Acknowledgement)
A reply sent from one computer to another. When one computer sends a block of data to another via a network, the second computer sends a reply *ACK* message indicating that the transfer of data has been carried out successfully, i.e. that the data has arrived at its destination free of errors. If errors are detected in transmission, the second computer can send a negative ACK message, or NAK.
See PING, XMODEM

National Center for Supercomputing Applications
See NCSA

National Science Foundation Network
See NSFNET

navigate, navigation
To move through web pages using *hypertext*.

NCSA (National Center for Supercomputing Applications)

NCSA™

An organisation belonging to the University of Illinois that developed the first graphic navigator, *Mosaic*, in 1992. It was one of the five original 'NSF Supercomputer Centres', known as the NSF Partnership for Advanced Computational Infrastructure (PACI), and in October 1997, it became one of the two partners of the National Computational Science Alliance (known as 'The Alliance'). The Alliance includes over 50 American academic members who are building the prototype for the country's future information and computer infrastructure. The NCSA's website is at www.ncsa.uiuc.edu

negative acknowledgement
See NAK

Neoplanet

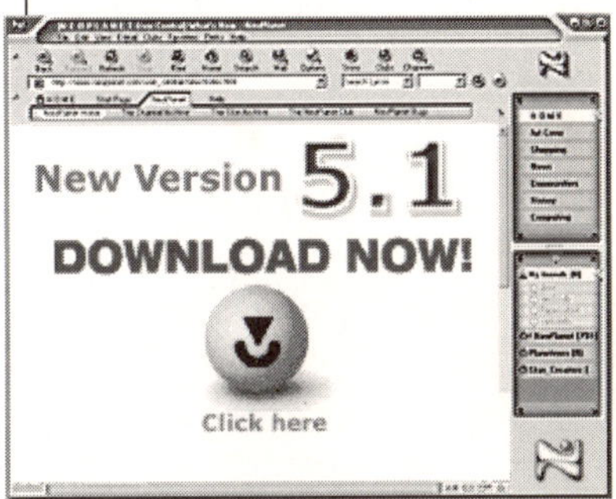

Free software that requires little hard disk space (less than 3MB). It expands the functions of the browser, enabling the creation of personalised screen designs, known as skins, or the downloading of many predefined designs from its website. Other interesting improvements have also been added.
It runs on Windows with Internet *Explorer* version 3.02, and will soon run with *Netscape*. The website is at www.neoplanet.com

.net
A *domain name* suffix. This is one of the domains available when a domain field is requested. The websites that use this domain name usually correspond to services related to computer networks; '.net' is an abbreviation of 'network'. An example is www.internic.net.

Net
Abbreviation of *Internet*.

Net Nanny
Software that prevents children from accessing pornographic material. It also prevents children's personal information, their telephone numbers or addresses, from circulating on the Internet.

netiquette
A combination of the words 'net' and 'etiquette', it refers to Internet etiquette, i.e. the unwritten rules of behaviour on the Internet, especially related to the use of *e-mail*, *chat rooms* and *USENET* newsgroups. It usually refers to comments or actions that are considered inappropriate or offensive.
See FLAME, MODERATOR

netizen
A combination of the words 'Internet' and 'citizen'. Being an Internet citizen implies that a person is civil in their use of the Internet and complies with its rules of behaviour.

Netscape
The usual way of referring to the Californian company Netscape Communications, which is mainly known for its browser Netscape Navigator. This and Microsoft Internet *Explorer* are the most widely used browsers on the Internet. Navigator was developed by Mark Andressen (originally from the *NCSA*) in 1995, and was based on *Mosaic*; the subsequent versions that have appeared on the market have made it a standard point of reference on the Internet. Version 4.0 is known as Netscape Communicator; this can be downloaded from Netscape's website at www.netscape.com
In 1999, Netscape was acquired by *SUN* and *AOL*.

Netscape Application Program Interface
See NSAPI

Netscape Navigator, Navigator
Netscape's browser software.
See NETSCAPE

network computer (NC)
A computer whose sole purpose is to connect to a network, such as the Internet, and, as a result, does not have all the characteristics of normal PCs.

network
Hardware and software that makes the connection between several computers easier and which enables users to share resources. There are different types of network, depending on their geographic

scope, such as *LAN* (Local Area Network) or *WAN* (Wide Area Network).

Network File System
See NFS

Network Information Center
See NIC

Network News Transfer Protocol
See NNTP

Network of networks
One of the names given to the Internet, as it consists of millions of computers linked to one single network.
See INTERNET

Network Solutions
See NSI

Network Time Protocol
See NTP

newbie
A novice on the Internet. The word is supposed to have come from the name once given to new pupils in some English schools, but it is more likely to have been coined by users themselves.
See KNOWBIE

.news
A suffix indicating a 'news newsgroup', i.e. a higher category of the *USENET* newsgroups which specialises in its own subject. Other categories of newsgroup are .alt (alternative), .comp (computer), .sci (science), .talk, .biz (business), .misc (miscellaneous), .rec (recreational) or .soc (social). These newsgroups can be accessed via the majority of Internet browsers.
See NEWSGROUPS

news server
A computer that controls the *newsgroup* service. From here, users can download the newsgroups they are interested in.

newsgroups, news, USENET
newsgroups, USENET News

Messages related to ~g rec.motorcycles:
Messages 1-25 of exactly 14757 matches

Date	Subject	Forum	Author
08/31/00	Re: Let me have it guys.....	rec.motorcycles	NZMSC
08/31/00	Re: I brought it home, and s	rec.motorcycles	csoto
08/31/00	Re: ZRX1100 - impressions???	rec.motorcycles	csoto
08/31/00	Re: New bike vibrates	rec.motorcycles	csoto
08/31/00	Re: sad over Nomad..girlfrie	rec.motorcycles	csoto
08/31/00	Re: sad over Nomad..girlfrie	rec.motorcycles	csoto
08/31/00	I managed to get the new bik	rec.motorcycles	Corsair
08/31/00	Re: Neutral light comes on w	rec.motorcycles	Linda
08/31/00	Dealer in P.A....They did ri	rec.motorcycles	Bilbo
08/31/00	Re: sad over Nomad..girlfrie	rec.motorcycles	DJ Jazzy Jett
08/31/00	Re: Motorcyclist Crashes, an	rec.motorcycles	Big Bob
08/31/00	Re: I brought it home, and s	rec.motorcycles	Holly Ober
08/31/00	Re: Dealer in P.A....They di	rec.motorcycles	Igli
08/31/00	Re: I managed to get the new	rec.motorcycles	Timberwoof
08/31/00	Transalp - Will it ever be b	rec.motorcycles	Bob Lovejoy

Systems that appeared long before the Internet became popular. The USENET newsgroups were the forums for discussion in USENET, offered as a service to clients by the *ISPs*. Participants discuss specific subjects, ask related questions and make impartial comments; they may take part in already existing groups or create new groups, as well as subscribe to those they are interested in. Occasionally, groups are moderated by people who screen out inappropriate contributions to the groups. There are thousands of groups with all kinds of topics being discussed by *surfers* from all around the world. The groups are placed in a hierarchy and represented by the first three or four letters of the word that describe them, preceded by a dot. For example:

.alt alternative: covers topics as varied as energy, drugs or the Esperanto language
.comp computer: computer-related topics
.news news: related to newsgroups
.sci science: topics on science, such as agriculture, biology or chemistry
.talk debates: discussions on philosophy, politics or religion
.biz business: related to commerce.
.rec recreational: related to leisure, such as sports, food and drink or games
.soc social: covers social topics, such as the elderly, women or atheism

Each group is divided into subgroups, for example 'comp.arch' is the computer architecture newsgroup or 'rec.sport.soccer' the football group; each message included in the group is called an 'article', which is identified by its title or 'subject line'. When a subgroup is accessed, all the titles are shown, with the aim of quickly identifying the information. Messages are also grouped in 'threads', which are messages linked to the same topic.
Newsgroups usually include a list of *FAQs* (Frequently Asked Questions) intended to answer beginners' doubts. The software used to take part in the newsgroups is called *Newsreader*. The example shows the messages sent to a newsgroup about motorbikes in '.rec'.

Newsreader
Software that enables users to interact with the *USENET newsgroups*, for reading and sending out messages, subscribing, etc. Many of the current browsers include newsreader functions.

Next Generation Internet
An initiative of the American government, aimed at developing the Internet of the future, its advanced applications and network requirements. This should not be confused with *Internet2*, with which it works closely in many fields.

NFS (Network File System)
A UNIX protocol developed by *Sun Microsystems* that enables saved files to be used in another computer as if they were in the originating computer.

NIC (Network Information Center)
A research centre that handles network information, for example, *InterNIC*, which registers domain names.

nickname
See ALIAS

NNTP (Network News Transfer Protocol)
A standard protocol that enables messages to be transferred in the *USENET newsgroups* through a *TCP/IP* network.

node
Equipment connected to the Internet, such as a PC, also called the *host*. Computers that provide services (such as *FTP*) are called *servers*.

non-graphic browser
See TEXT-BASED BROWSER

NSAPI (Netscape Application Program Interface)
The *API* included in *Netscape* server products. Have a look at www.networksolutions.com

NSFNET (National Science Foundation Network)
A government agency that created the *backbone* of the present Internet, for educational and scientific purposes, and which has now been disbanded. The NSF founded *Network Solutions Inc.*, which maintains the *domain* database for the entire network.

NSFNET Mid-Level
The network connected to *NSFNET* that covers a geographic area of the USA, also known as a regional network.

NSI (Network Solutions)
A company owned by *VeriSign* which exclusively registered the high-level domains '.org', '.net' and '.com', through an agreement with the government of the United States, which ended in September 2000. Since then, new companies have entered the market to carry out that function. By mid-2000, 12 million domains had already been registered.

NTP (Network Time Protocol)
A protocol used to synchronise clocks among Internet computers.

offline

The opposite to *online*, not being connected to a network or the Internet.

online

The opposite to *offline*. When a user is connected to the Internet, he/she is described as being online. This can also refer to Internet resources, such as online magazine, online dictionary, etc.

online database

A database that can be accessed via the Internet.

online newspaper

The New York Times Online STORE

The New York Times ON THE WEB

NYC Weather 74° F

THURSDAY, AUGUST 31, 2000 | Site Updated 12:22 PM

E-Mail Updates

QUICK NEWS
PAGE ONE PLUS
SITE INDEX
International
National/N.Y.
Politics
Business
Technology
Science/Health
Sports
Weather

Clinton to Veto a G.O.P. Bill To Repeal Federal Estate Tax

By JULIAN E. BARNES
NYT UPDATE, 11:30 A.M.

President Clinton is expected to veto a Republican-drafted bill that would repeal the estate tax. White House officials have said that the legislation will undermine the government's ability to pay down the national debt.

(AP)
Fire engulfed an unfinished condominium complex in

Internet newspapers are probably the websites that have developed most. They require a great deal of investment, given that they are updated daily, and the adaptation and amplification of their contents on paper requires a constantly working team of professionals. There are newspapers that operate both on paper and and in *cyberspace*, and newspapers that are exclusively edited on the Internet. One of the most interesting options offered by many newspapers is the possibility of personalising news information, i.e. establishing a reader profile that allows readers to assemble their own tailor-made newspaper.

Some of the most important newspapers that can be consulted on the Internet are the following:

www.wsj.com
The Wall Street Journal (United States)

www.nyt.com
The New York Times (United States)

www.washingtonpost.com
The Washington Post (United States)

www.sueddeutsche.de
Süddeutsche Zeitung (Germany)

www.toutlemonde.fr
Le Monde (France)

www.elpais.es
El País (Spain)

www.the-times.co.uk
The Times (Great Britain)

www.lastampa.it
La Stampa (Italy)

online service

A subscription service that provides access to the Internet, such as information services, *e-mail*, discussion groups, *chat rooms*, etc., for the exclusive use of its subscribers.

The best-known services are *America Online (AOL)*, *CompuServe* (acquired by AOL), Prodigy, *Delphi*, *Genie* and *The Microsoft Network*. A monthly fee is normally charged for using this service although some are free.

offline browser
Software that allows the user to view web pages without being connected to the Internet. These pages can generally be accessed if they are already on the computer's hard disk or an information storage system (CD-ROM, floppy disk).

Open Systems Interconnect
See OSI

Opera

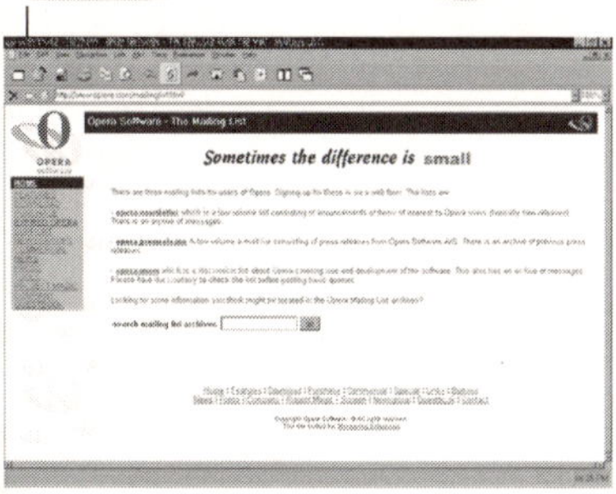

A browser created by Opera Soft, a Norwegian company based in Oslo, whose main characteristic is that it requires very little disk space (less than 2MB). This means it can be used in older, less powerful machines or in computers whose capacity is used for other functions. It has been updated with the new facilities, such as graphics format, multimedia, *XML*, *SSL*, the latest versions of *HTML*, etc.
It was created in 1992 and developed by a group of researchers from Telenor AS, the Norwegian telecommunications company. Telenor used the browser internally, but decided not to commercialise it. In 1998, it launched a shareware version available on the Internet. In 1999, over a million Opera browsers were *downloaded*. Its website is at www.opera.com

optical fibre
A method of transmitting light through fibre cables. The ray of light can modulate to transmit information. Fibre optics transmit the information quicker than other types of cable, and without information loss. This is different from transmission via electric impulse, as this method is subject to possible changes, caused by interference from electromagnetic waves, for example.

Oracle Corp.

A Californian company well known for its business software. It offers market-leading database products, tools and applications.

.org
A *domain*-name suffix. This is one of the domains that can be chosen when a domain field is requested. The websites that use this domain name are usually those belonging to non-profit-making organisations, non-governmental organisations or other types of organisations, for example, www.mozilla.org, www.congress.org, www.science.org.

OSI (Open Systems Interconnect)
A group of protocols created to be the standard international method of connection in computer networks.

packet

A block of data that is transmitted from one computer to another via the Internet. The *TCP/IP* protocol divides information into several packets, and each of these contains part of the data, an error identifier, sender, destination and the packet identifier. When packets reach their destination, the protocol checks that all have arrived error free and the data is reassembled.

Packet InterNet Groper

See PING

packet switching

The delivery of data in *packets* to another area via a network. The data is divided into packets that include the identification and the destination address, which enables different routes to be used for the data to arrive at the same destination, where it is reassembled on arrival.

page, web page

A document generally created using *HTML* and referenced within a *URL*. Each website is made up of multiple pages containing information. Pages can be viewed using a browser, and can be made up of text, images, graphics, audio, video or animation. The user can move up and down the page using the side *scroll bar* and move to other web pages using the *links* contained in the page.

page impressions

See PAGE VIEW

page view, page impressions

A measurement used in website statistics which indicates the number of pages in a website that a user has downloaded from the server.
See HIT

password

A secret code, generally alphanumerical, that is used to access a specific Internet *server*, for example to access *e-mail*, the Internet or a subscription *website*. For example, a subscriber to a stock-exchange information service will have to type in an identification password to access this information.

password archive

A file where all the system-access passwords are stored.

Patagon

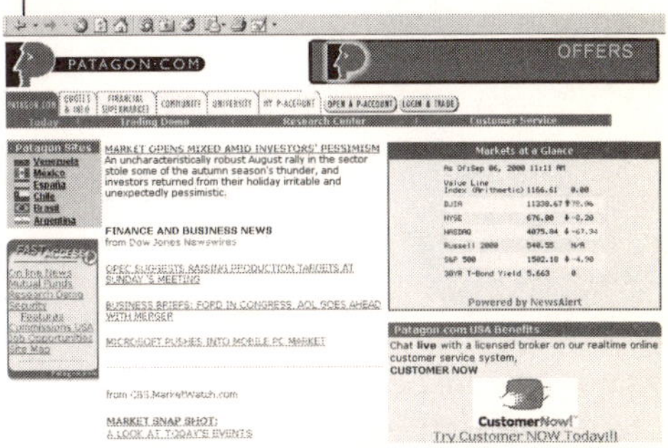

The main financial *portal* for Europe and Latin America, largely owned by BSCH (Banco Santander Central Hispano). Through this portal, financial products from the major banking institutions of each region can be accessed, online transactions can be made, and all the necessary information on financial markets and the global economy can be obtained.
Patagon was created in 1997 in Buenos Aires (Argentina) by two students who invested 30,000 dollars (all of their capital) with the aim of creating a service for buying and selling shares over the Internet. Over the next few years, they managed to attract the appropriate investment partners and started their expansion. In March 2000, the company was valued at 705 million dollars, having become the leader in the sector. Their website is at www.patagon.com

path, path name
The route that should be taken to access the desired web page.

PDA (Personal Digital Assistant)

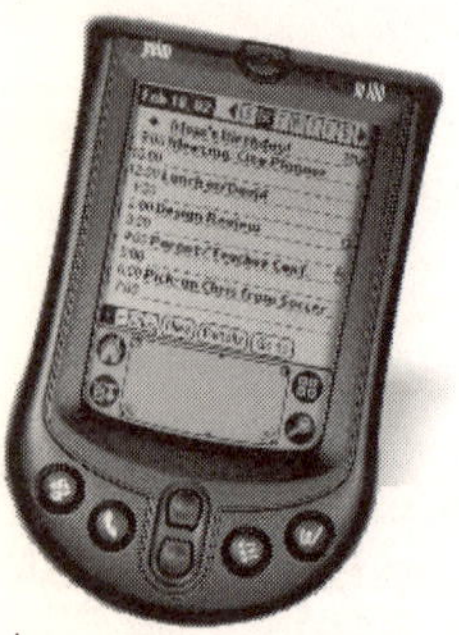

An alternative personal system to the laptop computer, PDAs are much smaller and generally fit into the palm of a hand. They usually combine functions ranging from a diary and telephone directory to telephone, fax and Internet access, spreadsheet and word-processing programs, etc. Well-known examples include Palm by 3Com, the palmtop with CE operating system, organisers with a built-in mobile telephone, etc. New, more sophisticated PDAs are constantly being produced.

PDF (Portable Document Format)
A format within the *Acrobat* software which enables users to create, save or view documents with the same appearance as the originals on any platform. The *Acrobat Reader* program is used to read these files. This can be used free by downloading it from the Adobe website (www.adobe.com) or from multiple links on the Internet. One of its main advantages is that it allows the user to save large documents as much smaller files, which are much easier to transmit quickly over the Internet.
Acrobat can run parallel to an Internet browser, or even as a *plug-in*, forming a part of the browser and opening documents within it.

Perl (Practical Extraction and Report Language)
A programing language developed by Larry Wall and used on the Internet to create *CGI* applications.

Petabyte
1 PB (Petabyte) = 1,000 Terabytes.
1 PBps = 1 Petabyte per second.
See BIT, BYTE

PGP (Pretty Good Privacy)
An encryption program developed by Phil Zimmermann which is very popular on the Internet. It allows the user to send and receive mail and documents without other users being able to read them. Another PGP characteristic is that digital signatures can be created on documents and mail as proof of identity, and these messages cannot be changed without this being detected by PGP.
It is one of the most secure systems that has been created.
See CERTIFYING AUTHORITY, ENCRYPTING, CRYPTOGRAPHY, DECODING, DIGITAL SIGNATURES

PGPI (Pretty Good Privacy International)
An international version of *PGP*, which differs slightly from the latter in that it supports RSA passwords and is available for more platforms, such as Amiga or several variations of UNIX. The website is at www.pgpi.com

ping (Packet Internet Groper)
One of the functions of the *TCP/IP* protocol, the ping is a message to check the connection with another Internet computer, or verify that the connection works correctly.
In this way, a specific host can be 'pinged' to check if it is working; it will send a reply message in return.

PKI (Public Key Infrastructure)
The public key system for transmitting encrypted data, which only the recipient of the message can open using their private key.
See CERTIFYING AUTHORITY, ENCRYPTING, CRYPTOGRAPHY, DECODING, DIGITAL SIGNATURES, PGP

PKZIP

A shareware compression tool for PCs that creates '.zip'-type documents. PKUNZIP is used to decompress these files.

plug-in
A software component that expands the capabilities of the browser (or other application), generally for reading or displaying specific types of documents that cannot otherwise be read. Some examples are Shockwave by Macromedia, *QuickTime* or *RealAudio*, which reads sound files.
The latest generation of browsers incorporate these plug-ins.

Point Of Presence
See POP

Point-to-Point Protocol
See PPP

POP (Point Of Presence)
A local telephone service accessed for connecting to the Internet. The larger Internet servers provide POPs, distributed all around the country, which have different telephone numbers that are accessed according to your geographical location.

Connecting to areas that are nearby means that the telephone charges are lower.

POP (Post Office Protocol)
A protocol for use between *e-mail* servers and clients. When messages are received, they are stored in the *ISP*'s server until they are accessed by users logging on, identifying themselves using the POP protocol and downloading the mail to read on their own computer. There are three versions: POP, POP2 and POP3, the latter being the most frequently used. The alternative to POP is *IMAP*, or Interactive Mail Access Protocol, with which mail can be read on the server without having to download it. This should not be confused with *SMTP*, which is the protocol used to transmit mail on the Internet; the mail is read from the server using POP or IMAP.

POP3 (Post Office Protocol 3)
See POP

POP Server
The server which receives and stores e-mail files.
See POP

Popmail
See POP

port
The part of the web server that fulfils requests for certain services, for example *Telnet*, *FTP*, *WWW*. Each one is assigned its own port number, for example the web servers use port 80, and if this is specified in the URL as http://www.business.com: 8000, then this indicates it is not in a standard port. *HTTPS* uses 443, *Gopher* uses 70, the e-mail server uses 110, *Telnet* uses 23, etc.
Users can access a particular port without the need to know the various numbers, as the system automatically selects the right one.

port number
See PORT

Portable Document Format
See PDF

portal
From the Latin 'porta' meaning 'doorway'. A portal gives access to all types of service, such as news, weather, search engines, games, e-mail, the stock exchange, geographic information, *chat rooms*, forums, etc. in the same way as an entrance hall gives access to the rooms of a house in the real world.
Sites which started off as directories and search engines have evolved into websites which include all kinds of information, including the sale of products and services, creating the portals as they are known today. A large number of portals have appeared recently, many of them developed by telecommunications companies, such as www.altavista.com, www.canal21.com, www.go.com, www.yahoo.com, www.excite.com, www.terra. com, www.ya.com, www.msn.com and www.lycos.com.

post
A message sent to a newsgroup or a mailing list that can be read by other users.
See POSTING

Post Office Protocol
See POP

posting

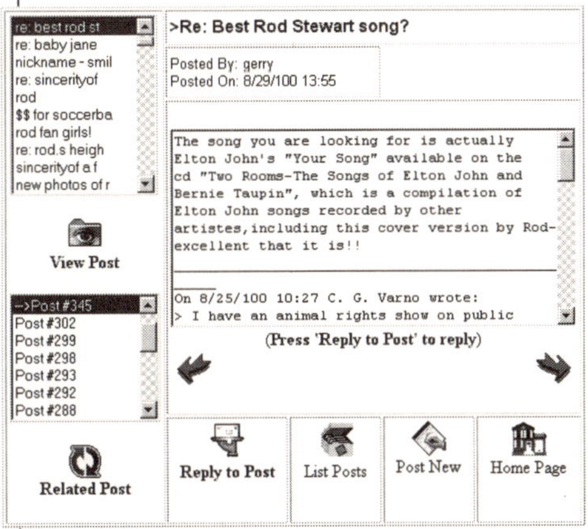

The sending of *post*. The example shows post placed on the message board of the company Warner Bros. Records, about the singer Rod Stewart.

postmaster
The person responsible for the maintenance of a mail server. The postmaster can generally be contacted via the e-mail address postmaster@company.com.

PPP (Point-to-Point Protocol)
A communications and package-sending protocol that enables the *TCP/IP* protocol to be used and which connects computers to the Internet via a modem and telephone line. PPP is the present alternative to *SLIP* (Serial Line Internet).

Practical Extraction and Report Language
See PERL

Pretty Good Privacy
See PGP

Pretty Good Privacy International
See PGPI

print button

A browser button for printing out the page being viewed. This function can also be activated from the menu bar of the browser.

protocol
Rules and regulations that are applied to carry out a specific function such as transferring data between two computers. Computers and networks communicate between themselves whilst adhering to standard protocols. Some of the most common on the Internet are:

- FTP — File Transmission Protocol
- IP Address — Internet Protocol Address
- TCP/IP — Transmission Control Protocol/Internet Protocol
- POP — Post Office Protocol
- HTTP — HyperText Transfer Protocol
- NNTP — Network News Transfer Protocol
- SMTP — Simple Mail Transfer Protocol

provider
See ISP (INTERNET SERVICE PROVIDER)

proxy
See PROXY SERVER

proxy server
An Internet security system. When a proxy server is used, requests are sent to Internet servers throughout the system, instead of sending them directly from one computer.

PSTN (Public Switched Telephone Network)
A telephone network for transmitting voice and data.

public domain
Software free of patents and copyrights, which can be used freely without paying or requesting authorisation from its creators.

Public Key Infrastructure
See PKI

publishing
The act of placing information on an Internet server so that it can be accessed by *surfers*. It is much easier to publish on the Internet than via traditional means.

pull
When someone searches for, requests and accesses information on the Internet. The opposite is *push*.

pure player
A business that operates solely on the Internet, i.e. it does not come from a business in the real world.
See CLICK AND MORTAR

push
When information is sent to users without them having to search for it. This happens when users subscribe to certain services and indicate the type of information that they would like to receive. The information usually relates to news, weather, sports or the stock exchange.
The opposite is *pull*, when it is the user who searches the Internet for information. Products for pushing are PointCast and Marimba.

push media
Push technology that sends news.

Quake
One of the games that has most revolutionised the sector. It consists of annihilating the enemy in a 3D environment. On the Internet, it can be played against other users (multiplayer). Its website is at www.quake.com

query
A search request sent to a database to locate particular information or all the results coinciding with the criteria being searched for. A query is made up of one or several words – occasionally sentences – which can have the words 'or', 'and' or 'not' between them in order to better define the search.
See BOOLEAN OPERATOR

QuickTime

A multi-platform, multimedia format developed by Apple Computers that can include text, graphics, sound, music, animation, video and even 360° virtual-reality scenes.
It is supplied as standard with the Apple Macintosh operating system.
It appeared in 1991, and at present is one of the most popular on the Internet. The website is at www.apple.com/quicktime

Gladiator
Copyright © 2000 DreamWorks Pictures

QuickTime Live Keynote

QuickTime VR

Virtual-reality technology from Apple that can be used on Windows and Macintosh. The sofware uses photographs and computer-generated images to represent virtual worlds with a real 3D appearance where the user can turn 360° and shift between scenes at a click of the mouse. On the Internet, it is used as a browser *plug-in* which enables pages created with this software to be included in and viewed on thousands of websites. The website is at www.apple.com/quicktime/qtvr

real time
Now, in the present. A real-time conversation is when the messages being written immediately appear on other monitors connected to the Internet. Real-time video is when pictures are transmitted over the Internet of events as they actually happen.
See WEBCAM

RealAudio

A *plug-in* from the Progressive Networks company which lets users reproduce audio files with the '.rm' extension as they are being downloaded. This means that it is not necessary to download the whole document before it can be listened to. This process is called *streaming*.

RealJukebox

Jukebox software that allows the user to create and combine lists of digitalised music and reproduce *MP3* files.

RealMedia
See REALPLAYER

RealNetworks

A company founded by Rob Glaser, pioneer and leader in sending multimedia via the Internet. His first product, *RealPlayer,* was launched in 1995, and by mid-2000, it had over 130 million registered users, increasing by 200,000 users per day. His other well-known product, *RealJukebox*, was launched in May 1999, and by mid-2000 had 35 million users, making it the most popular jukebox software in North American homes.
Amongst other characteristics, RealNetworks products allow users to view live sports, music, news and recreational events, as well as to download stored contents that can be viewed as they are being downloaded, without having to wait until downloading has been completed. The website is at www.realnetworks.com

RealPlayer

A *plug-in* that offers sufficient quality to view video, accompanied by high-quality audio. RealPlayer adjusts its speed cha-

racteristics to the computer on which it is loaded and can display video at the same time that it is being downloaded. This is an advantage over almost all other current Internet systems, which require the sequence to be completely downloaded before it can be viewed. This process is called *streaming*. RealPlayer can be downloaded from www.real.com.

.rec (rec newsgroup)
A higher category of the USENET *newsgroups* specialising in leisure subjects (recreational).
Other categories of newsgroups are .alt (alternative), .news, .comp (computer), .sci (science), .biz (business), .talk and .soc (social).
These newsgroups can be accessed via the majority of Internet browsers.
See NEWSGROUPS

refresh button
See RELOAD BUTTON

reload button, refresh button

A browser button that reloads the page on view. It is normally used when part of the page has been downloaded with errors (for example, an image that does not appear) or when it is a page that changes every so often (for example, stock-exchange quotations).

remote access
Access to a computer located elsewhere, i.e. not a local network. Remote access requires specific hardware and communications software, as well as access to a telephone line. The greatest problem presented by remote access is that connections are generally slower, especially when access is via a *modem*. The problem is made worse when large files are being transferred. It does, however, enable users to access remote servers at relatively low cost.

Request For Comments
See RFC

response time
The period of time that elapses between a request being sent to an Internet server and the requested information being received.

RFC (Request For Comments)
A series of Internet research and development documents. These are used to define and establish Internet standards and protocols and are accompanied by a number, such as RFC-822 which defines the standards for *e-mail*. They come under the responsibility of the *IETF* (Internet Engineering Task Force) and can be downloaded from *FTP* anonymously.

ring, web ring, webring

A group of websites linked together that have a common theme (for example, when they all deal with *webcams*). There are already hundreds or possibly thousands of rings on every subject, such as games, computers, cars, etc. These websites are catalogued in a server and, by using the links that connect them, users can *surf* through them all, until they get back to the first one, hence the name 'ring'. Many rings have additional characteristics, such as random website hits, or a list of all websites to enable users to directly access the one they want.
One of the best known and first to appear was www.webring.org, created by Sage Weil in March 1995, and operated since August 1997 by WebRing Inc. At present, it is one of the most visited, and in 2000, it was made up of more than 80,000 rings, more than 1,300,000 websites and two million pages visited every day.
The example shows the 'Live WebCams Ring', which brings together more than 1,800 webcams from all around the world. Using the menu, users can move through them one after the other or at random.

Rio
The Diamond Rio PMP300 device was the first *MP3* player to appear on the market. It is much smaller than the typical walkman (it fits into the palm of a hand), weighs 70 grams and has high sound quality. It can store an hour of sound (32MB flash memory) and allows users convert songs from standard CD into MP3 format. It can incorporate *plug-in* memory cards to store more music. Recently, many other players have appeared on the market, but Rio was the first. The website is at www.riohome.com

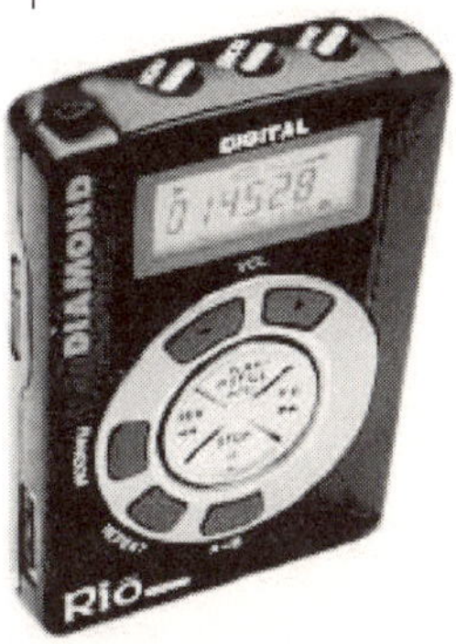

RIPE NCC
A non-profit-making organisation created to administer and register *IP addresses* (Internet Protocol) in the geographical areas of Europe, the Middle East and regions of Africa. It is one of the three worldwide Regional Internet Registries that jointly provide registration services throughout the world.
See ARIN, APNIC

robot
See SPIDER

router
A communications device that manages data between two or more networks. Routers read the destination addresses of *packets* and decide on the route to send them so that they arrive at the correct address. Networks use *IP (Internet Protocol)*.

routing
The process of sending a message via a network or between networks via the most suitable route.

RSA Security
A company based in Massachusetts and recognised for the advances it has made in Internet security, especially in encryption and public-key topics.
Its website is at www.rsasecurity.com

RTF (Rich Text Format)
A text document format developed by Microsoft for exchanging documents between applications.
It is especially useful when sending text documents between platforms, p.g. PC to Mac.

.sci (science newsgroup)
A higher category of the USENET *newsgroups* specialising in sciences, especially in areas such as agriculture, biology and chemistry.
Other categories of newsgroups are .alt (alternative), .news, .comp (computer), .talk, .biz (business), .misc (miscellaneous), .rec (recreational) and .soc (social).
These newsgroups can be accessed via the majority of Internet browsers.
See NEWSGROUPS

scroll bar
Used to move around the page, up and down (right bar) and from left to right (lower bar). Scroll bars are generally found on the right side and at the bottom of the browser screen. The long bars are used for scrolling quickly, and the small squares with the arrows for moving around more slowly.

search button

A button on the browser for carrying out searches.

search engine
A tool for locating documents, generally web pages, by entering keywords. When the search is complete, the search engine lists the documents found, including links to these. The documents can be accessed by clicking on these links. Search engines usually have a tool for dragging the Internet for new websites to be included in their database. These are called *bots* (robots), *spiders* or *crawlers*.
See SEARCHER

searcher
Software that lets users find pages and websites on the Internet through consulting databases. More generally, this term has a wider meaning, referring both to websites as well as to areas within these destined to carry out searches on the Internet in general. The searches are carried out using keywords. When the Internet started to grow out of all proportion, and the number of websites made it almost impossible to locate the information being sought, individuals and small companies started to appear on the scene that created lists (or directories). In these directories, the different websites were classified by subject, and later on they also incorporated search engines. Many websites include both a directory as well as a search engine.
There are search engines that locate websites, and others that locate specific pages within websites. There are also specialised search engines that locate information on specific topics (such as golf or companies). Other search engines incorporate the contents of *newsgroups*.
Search engines are fed information sent to them by those in charge of websites, generally by filling in a form included on

the search-engine page. They also use robots, bots (abbreviation of 'robot'), *spiders* or crawlers, which surf the Internet in search of new websites, or deleting sites that have disappeared from the database. When robots carry out a search and classify websites, they usually pay special attention to the words used in the title and to the descriptions and keywords that are added in the metatags at the beginning of the pages. These metatags are not usually seen when the page is shown in the browser, but they are seen when the *HTML* codes are shown. Other search engines base their classification on the number of times the words appear on the page. There are also manual searches, where people classify pages.

The best-known search engines have begun to change their structure to the point that they have become *portals*, adding contents and selling products and services. This is the case of the exemplary search engine, *Yahoo*.

Search engines usually include advice for productive searching on their pages, but it is useful to bear the following in mind:

- Write words in lower-case letters, except those that always start with a capital letter (like surnames).
- Use several search engines, as no single search engine contains all the websites on the Internet.
- Refine the search using various words with *Boolean operators*. If only one word is entered, there could be hundreds or thousands of responses. Examples of this are:
  - Put inverted commas around specific phrases, e.g. 'latest generation mobile telephones'.
  - Put a plus sign before words that should appear in the search result (e.g. History + England), or a minus sign or 'and not' if a word should not appear (e.g. History — England).
  - 'And' indicates that both terms should appear in the results (History and England), 'or' that at least one of the words should appear, and 'near' that the terms should appear near each other.

Examples of search engines:

- www.excite.com
- www.yahoo.com
- www.webcrawler.com
- www.infoseek.com
- www.lycos.com
- www.altavista.com
- www.hotbot.com
- www.terra.com

These are some of the best-known search engines, containing millions of websites and Internet pages, but there are thousands on the Internet, and there are even websites with lists of general as well as specialist search engines.

The next example shows an advanced search engine in *Yahoo*.

See BOOLEAN

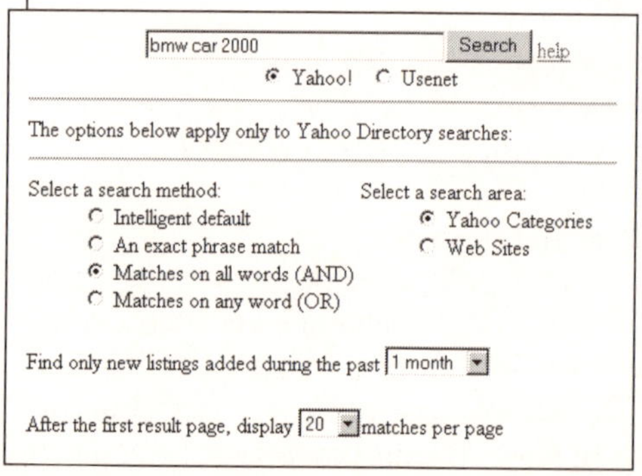

Secure Electronic Transaction
See SET

Secure Hypertext Transfer Protocol
See HTTPS

secure server
A server that uses the *SSL* (Secure Sockets Layer) protocol to encrypt data that is transferred on *TCP/IP* networks.
See HTTPS

Secure Sockets Layer
See SSL

security
Security on the Internet refers to the control mechanisms established to avoid inappropriate or non-authorised use of systems. This can cover very different aspects:
- Access security to some services or restricted areas. Generally controlled using a password.
- System security, maintained by the System Administrator or SysAdmin.
- Security against viruses which could enter the system.
- Security in *e-business* payments.
- Security in information *encryption*.
- Security in *e-mails*.

Serial Line Internet Protocol
See SLIP

server
A computer which receives a request from *surfers* and supplies information such as *HTML* pages, *e-mail* or files. The *ISPs* usually have different servers for different functions, e.g. a web-page server, e-mail server, *FTP* server, etc.
When pages are downloaded onto a PC, they come from a web server.

SET (Secure Electronic Transaction)
The standard protocol for transactions made using credit cards, developed in 1995 by a consortium formed by Visa, MasterCard, *VeriSign*, *Microsoft*, *Netscape*, *RSA* and other leading technology companies.
SET was designed to make payments and online transactions secure, authenticating all parties involved in the transaction. It was also intended to offer a standard format for transmitting confidential payment information.
The user receives a digital certificate and, when the transaction is carried out, this is verified using a combination of certificates and digital signatures between the purchaser, his or her financial institution and the seller.
The main difference between SET and *SSL* is that this system guarantees the identity of the parties taking part in the transaction. At present, SET is backed by organisations such as banks and other financial institutions, credit-card companies and high-tech companies.
The SET certificates can belong to card holders, shop owners and Payment Channels.
A SET *e-business* transaction is carried out as follows:
- The purchaser connects to the shop's website via a browser.
- The purchaser selects a product that she/he wants to buy.

- The purchaser sees a purchase-request form which contains a list of products, prices, taxes, shipping costs, etc. This request form could be sent from the shop's server or created by the cardholder's own e-business purchasing software.
- The purchaser selects from the means of payment offered by the shop. If the 'credit-card payment using SET' option is selected, this *wallet* will be opened.
- From her/his wallet, the purchaser selects the SET certificate linked to the card with which she/he wants to make the payment.
- Communication under the SET protocol is established between the browser and the shop using the SET certificates of the purchaser and the shop.
- The purchaser, using her/his wallet, sends out two envelopes with the certificate information: the signed purchase order (open message) and a signed payment order (encrypted).
- The shop receives the electronic transaction from the purchaser and verifies, through their management software, the validity of the purchaser's certificate and the purchase order signed by the purchaser.
- The shop sends the transaction data and the encrypted envelopes with the purchaser's card details to the Payment Channel.
- The Payment Channel receives the electronic transaction and verifies the certificates of the signatures of the shop and the purchaser. It then decodes the authorisation order sent by the shop and the card details sent by the purchaser with the purpose of requesting economic authorisation from the corresponding Means of Payment.
- The Payment Channel processes the economic authorisation request from the corresponding Means of Payment.
- The Means of Payment authorises the payment and sends a message with the SET transaction authorisation number to the Payment Channel.
- The Payment Channel sends the SET authorisation number to the shop.
- The shop sends the products or provides the requested services.
- The Means of Payment carries out payment to the shop or service provider and charges the purchase to the purchaser.

See WALLET

set-top box

Equipment connected to a television and to telephone lines, a satellite dish or cable for the purpose of *surfing*, using e-mail, home shopping, etc.

See WebTV

SGML (Standard Generalized Markup Language)

The international standard established in 1986 for the description of electronic mark-up text. This is a metalanguage, and *HTML* and *XML* have been developed from it.

shareware

Software that can be used free for a limited trial period (normally a month), after which a small amount of money should be paid for its use. This is usually software created by independent programers

or small companies. Some shareware does not include all the functions until the licence has been paid, at which time all the documents, instruction manuals and technical support become available.
Not to be confused with *freeware*, which is free software with no time limitations.

Shockwave Flash
See FLASH

Shockwave player
Macromedia software that shows multimedia on the Internet. It is used for games, interactive creations, recreational and cultural topics and training. The player is free and can be downloaded from www.macromedia.com/shockwave.

shopping cart

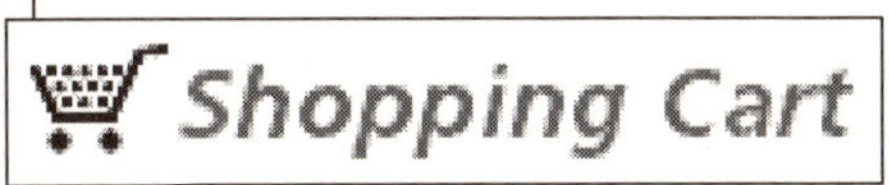

A virtual shopping trolley. The term comes from traditional supermarkets and is used in practically all Internet shops. Users opt to put products they want to buy into their shopping cart as they surf the shop's website. It can be viewed at any time by clicking on the trolley icon to check what has been added, and items that are no longer required can be removed. Almost all *e-business* software incorporates a shopping cart, and on many occasions this is represented by an icon of a real shopping trolley.
Certain websites store information on customers' shopping habits with the aim of saving them time when selecting these products. This is typical in virtual supermarkets where the regular shopping list usually changes very little.

shouting
Writing something in capital letters when participating in *newsgroups*, *chat rooms* or when writing e-mail. Text written ALL IN CAPS is like shouting at the other person, denoting annoyance or anger.

SHTTP
See HTTPS

SIG (Special Interest Group)
A discussion group through e-mail, *IRC* channels or networks. Also known as *forum*.

signature, .sig, signature file, .sig file
Digital text placed at the end of the message, in ASCII code form, which includes information on the author of the mail or *newsgroup* message, such as position, company name, telephone number, web address, etc. Some systems allow this information to be automatically included when mail is sent, in other cases it is included manually. It is also common to find drawings created with ASCII characters used to spell out the person's signature.

An example of a signature is:
John Smith
Marketing Director
Oquendos, Inc.
www.oquendos.com

Silicon Alley
An area of Manhattan (New York) in which a large number of Internet companies are based. The name is used in reference to the famous *Silicon Valley* in California.

Silicon Valley
The geographic area of California where many leading computer companies are based.

Simple Mail Transport/Transfer Protocol
See SMTP

Simple Network Management Protocol
See SNMP

site
See WEBSITE

SLIP (Serial Line Internet Protocol)
A standard, although not on the Internet, used for point-to-point connections on the *TCP/IP* protocol; the predecessor of *PPP* (Point-to-Point Protocol). SLIP defines a sequence of characters that structures IP *packets* in a series.

smart card
A plastic card similar in appearance to a credit card, which contains an electronic memory and, occasionally, an integrated circuit with a microprocessor. Smart cards can be used to identify the cardholder and store user information, the validity of PINs (personal identity numbers), authorisation of purchases, etc. They can also be used to ensure secure Internet transactions.

smiley
See EMOTICON

SMTP (Simple Mail Transport/ Transfer Protocol)
A standard protocol that uses *TCP/IP* and controls the exchange of messages through Internet servers, specifying how two mail systems interact. This means complying with the regulations on how a program that sends mail should act with another program that receives mail. When mail is sent, it goes first to an SMTP server, and from there to the SMTP server of the recipient.

snail mail
A pejorative term coined by Internet users to talk about traditional mail, compared with *e-mail*. The term is frequently used in the United States to refer to the United States Postal Service. Its detractors use the argument that e-mail reaches the other side of the globe in scarcely a few seconds, in comparison with the days taken by traditional mail.

SNMP (Simple Network Management Protocol)
A protocol used to manage nodes and network devices based on *TCP/IP*; it generally hosts, hubs and *routers*.

.soc (soc newsgroup)
A higher category of the USENET *newsgroups* specialising in social topics, such as the elderly, women or atheism.
Other categories of newsgroups are .alt (alternative), .news, .comp (computer), .sci (science), .biz (business), .misc (miscellaneous), .rec (recreational) or .talk.
These newsgroups can be accessed via the majority of Internet browsers without the need for additional specialist software.
See NEWSGROUPS

socket
The combination of an *IP server* address and a *port*, for example, 209.102.109.20 port 80. This allows connection to another active program in another computer connected to the Internet.

sound files
Digitalised files that, when activated, reproduce voice or music. The most standard audio file formats are the following:
- audio only files: .au, .mid, .wav
- audio and video files: .avo, .mov, .mpg, qt (*QuickTime*)

sound player
An application added to a browers which allows the reproduction of *sound files*.

source document
An HTML document, based on text, which contains the commands necessary for a browser to show the requested web page on screen. As a result, the page being viewed on the browser usually has a document created in HTML as a source.

spam

Junk mail or inappropriate mail, generally commercial and unsolicited, sent to *bulletin boards*, *newsgroups*, mailing lists or e-mail addresses. When junk mail is sent to e-mail addresses, this is usually done with a large number of identical messages to Internet users' mailing lists. The same message can be sent thousands of times to different users. This behaviour is poorly regarded within the Internet community, as it breaks one of the basic rules of *netiquette*.
The reaction of *surfers* is usually to send response messages with a large document attached which blocks the original mail server, and make the *ISP* lower the quality of its services to other clients. The verb is 'spamming'.
The word 'spam' comes from a parody by Monty Python which takes place in the Green Midget Café, in which the word 'spam' is repeated many times. Its relationship with Spam, a spiced pork sandwich-filling made by Hormel, is more dubious. Hormel was founded in Austin, Minnesota in 1937 and is still successfully selling its product, available in 12-ounce tins.
Hormel's website is at www.spam.com, where you will find allusions to its relationship with Monty Python.

spamming
The action of sending out *spam*.

Special Interest Group
See SIG

spider, robot, crawler, bot
A *search engine* which begins in a web page and then accesses each link, visiting the linked pages and theoretically reviewing all the pages present on Internet. It stores all the *URLs* visited and enters these into a database, putting them in-order. It either starts with keywords on web pages or lists all the words that appear. It often creates an index based on the metatags in the title. The Internet has become so vast that there is no single search engine which contains every single web page in order, especially given that the rate of growth in the number of new pages and changes to existing pages is phenomenal. Spiders are used to create and maintain commercial search engines.
There are several specialised search engines which scan the Internet in search of e-mail addresses or copyright violations.

spidering
The process of searching for web pages on the Internet.
See SPIDER

SQL (Structured Query Language)
A standard programing language which specialises in extracting, modifying or deleting information from related databases.

SSL (Secure Sockets Layer)

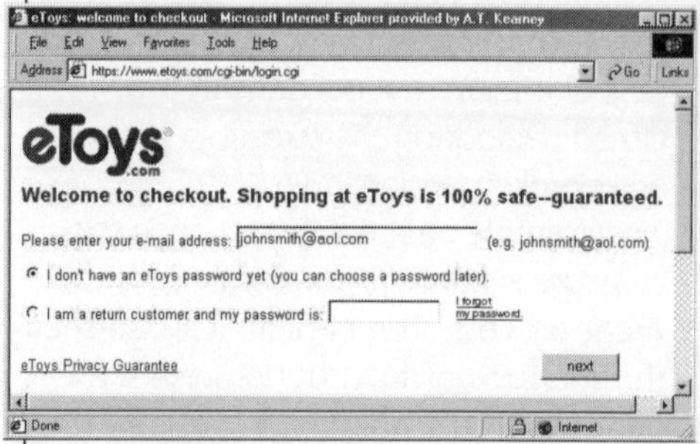

The standard security protocol for securing the transmission of data between computer networks. At present, this is very widely used on the Internet and has helped the rapid growth of *e-business*, as it enables encrypted, secure and complete transactions using credit cards in many Internet businesses. It also has the advantage that it can be used to carry out other types of secure operations. Measures such as this are necessary on the Internet, as data travels through many computers before reaching its destination, and other users could access this information.
If a web page offers secure transmission of data, the initials *HTTPS* appear; the 's' indicates an SSL connection is being used. The procedure is quite simple: both computers are sent a security certificate. The information sent (payment details, etc.) is then encrypted using information from both certificates, so that only the authorised recipient can open the document and read the decoded information. It uses the *RSA* public and private key encryption system and a digital *certificate*. SSL was developed by the Californian

company *Netscape* Communications Corp. The browser itself shows whether or not a secure connection has been set up. In the case of Microsoft, this is done by showing a closed padlock on the screen; in Netscape, an unbroken key is shown.

The example on the previous page shows a secure web page for the 'e Toys' payment process. The padlock can be seen in the lower right-hand part of the browser and the *URL* shown is https://www.etoys.com/cgi-bin/login.cgi.

Standard Generalized Markup Language
See SGML

StarMedia

A *portal* with headquarters in New York. It was set up in 1996 and is aimed at the Spanish- and Portuguese-speaking market. It operates in Spain, Argentina, Brazil, Chile, Colombia, Mexico, Puerto Rico, Uruguay, Venezuela and the United States. Its website is at www.starmedia.com

status bar

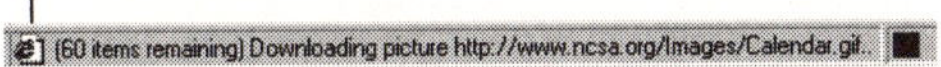

The bar at the bottom of the browser screen, underneath the *scroll bar*, which indicates the status of the command given to the browser. Some of the actions that can be shown are:

- When mail is being sent, the 'send' status is indicated with blocks progressively filling up the bar.
- When the cursor is moved over a link, the address of the link is shown.
- When a page search is in progress, the 'search' status is indicated so the user knows whether or not it is searching, if the page has been found and if it is being downloaded.

STN
See PSTN

stop button

A browser button which stops downloading the present page.

stream, streaming
The reproduction of audio, video or animation at the same time as the file is being downloaded from a remote Internet server. It is a much more advanced system than waiting for the complete file to be downloaded before playing it, which is especially tiresome when downloading large files. There are several programs that can be used to stream files, such as those by Real or Microsoft; in many cases, they allow the user to download part of the information in the buffer beforehand. This avoids gaps in the replay when breaks or speed reductions occur during transmission.

Documents are usually compressed to a very high degree so that they can be easily downloaded using modems of 28.8 or 14.4 Kbps. With high-velocity connections, and using *ADSL*, *ISDN* or cable modem, downloading is done very quickly, and the quality of the audio or video is usually much better. Many websites allow users to select the download speed, according to their modem; the higher the velocity, the better the quality.

streaming audio
Replaying audio files while the file is being downloaded.
See STREAM

streaming video
Replaying video files while the file is being downloaded.
See STREAM

Structured Query Language
See SQL

stuff, unstuff
The process of file compression (stuffing) and decompression (unstuffing). It is also known as zipping and unzipping.

StuffIt
A program for compressing and decompressing files, very popular with Macintosh users. The latest version is called StuffIt Deluxe.

subject
An e-mail message field located in the header, indicating the topic of the mail being sent.

subscribe
To become a member of a mailing list that enables the user to receive mail on topics of interest, or from a *newsgroup*, electronic newspaper, etc.

Sun Microsystems Inc.

A company set up in 1982 which launched *Java* in 1995 and *Jini* in 1998. In 1999, it reached a strategic agreement with *America Online Inc.*, creating iPlanet to provide e-business solutions.

surf
To navigate through the Internet. This term is used because users do not navigate linearly, but rather by using links, continually changing direction in an undefined manner. A user can be said to be surfing when he/she is navigating erratically with no clear direction.

surfer
An Internet user who *surfs*.

surfing
The process of navigating through the Internet using a browser.

SurfWatch

A company that started out in May 1995 offering Internet filtering products. It was bought by Spyglass Inc. in April 1996 and again in November 1999 by JSB Software Technologies. Its products filter *IRC* contents, *newsgroups*, websites and other areas of the *World Wide Web*.

The filters that it offers include five main categories:

- drugs, alcohol and tobacco
- gambling
- bad language
- sex
- violence

SurfWatch blocks access to millions of websites, 5,000 newsgroups and 200 *chat* channels.

Its programs are often used by parents who want to prevent their children from accessing certain areas of the Internet where the topics are unsuitable, for example pornography.

Its website is at www.surfwatch.com

Sybase

A company well known for its *SQL* database and middleware products. Its website is at www.sybase.com

sysop (Systems Operator)

The person in charge of controlling and operating a *bulletin-board system*, website, *forum*, *newsgroup*, *LAN*, etc.

T1
A high-speed, wide-band telephone connection which allows for data transfer at 1.544 million bits per seconds or 1.544 Mbps. It is the standard digital transmission system in the United States, Canada, Hong Kong and Japan.

T3
A telephone connection which allows for data transfer at 45 million bits per second or 44.736 Mbps, enough to transmit full-screen video.

tag
A term used in *HTML* page creation. Tags are format codes which indicate to the browser how the information should be displayed. For example, <br> indicates a line break and <p> denotes the beginning of a screen. They are invisible unless the HTML cod es are displayed.

.talk (talk newsgroup)
A major USENET *newsgroup* hierarchy devoted to subjects such as philosophy, politics or religion.
Other newsgroup categories are .alt (alternative), .news, .comp (computer), .sci (science), .biz (business), .misc (miscellaneous), .rec (recreational) or .soc (social). These newsgroups can be accessed through most Internet browsers.
See NEWSGROUPS

TCP (Transmission Control Protocol)
See TCP/IP

TCP/IP (Transmission Control Protocol/Internet Protocol)
A group of communication protocols which govern the basic operation of the Internet independently from existing operating systems. It forms the basis for information transmission and routing. It is also used in *Intranets* and Extranets. It was first used in 1983 by the US Defence Department. It is divided into two parts:

- TCP (Transmission Control Protocol) ensures that data is correctly transmitted between two computers. If information loss is experienced, it is re-sent. TCP is responsible for dividing messages into small data *packets*, sending them via the Internet, re-sending those which are lost or damaged and reassembling them correctly at their destination to re-create the original message.
- IP (Internet Protocol) indicates how data packets travel from their source to their destination via various routes. In order to do this, each packet indicates its destination address, and every computer through which it passes checks that address in order to send it correctly through the system.

Other well-known protocols are *FTP* (File Transfer Protocol), *HTTP* (Hypertext Transfer Protocol), *Telnet* and *SMTP* (Simple Mail Transfer Protocol). All of these protocols are bundled with TCP/IP as a suite. *UDP* (the transport protocol layer or User Datagram Protocol) is sometimes used in lieu of TCP.

Telnet
A standard Internet program and protocol which allows users to remotely access another computer anywhere in the world and use its files and programs if they have authorised access (for which a user ID and a *password* is usually required). It is a user command and a part of *TCP/IP*.
The source computers are usually large (workstations) and store data to which individuals might require access, for example in a research centre or a university. One of Telnet's uses is to allow participation in text-based games known as *MUD*.
Network and *FTP* protocols permit users to request specific files from remote computers, but do not register them as users. With Telnet, registered-user access is gained, with all of the previously authorised privileges.

Terabyte
1 TB (Terabyte) = 1,000 Gigabytes.
1Tbps = 1 Terabyte per second.
See BIT, BYTE

Terra

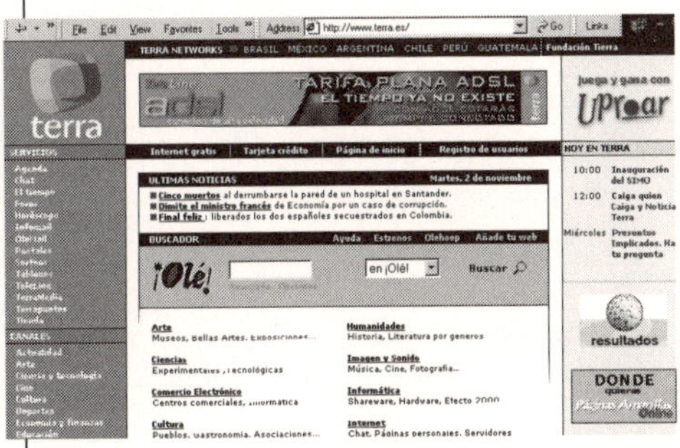

One of the world's largest *portals*. Specifically targeted at the Spanish-speaking world, in mid-2000 it reached an agreement with *Lycos*, becoming a global portal. It can be visited at www.terra.com

text-based browser
A browser which does not display hypermedia files, only text. These browsers are now obsolete, both due to the emergence of graphic browsers and the large number of web pages which use graphics. One example was the *Lynx* browser.

thread
The chain of messages in a USENET *newsgroup* and all responses related to that article, as well as responses to the responses. It allows users to follow responses to the initial article, select them, go to the next message or choose which message to go to. It usually refers to a topic. Responses and new messages are continually added to it from other participants who wish to put forth their ideas.

Three-Letter Acronym
See TLA

thumbnail
A small-sized, low-resolution image, seen when browsing web pages, which, when clicked on, opens a larger, higher-resolution image. There is usually an indication of this facility on the page. It enables complete pages with images to be downloaded quickly; any detailed images can be requested later. For example, when accessing a photographic archive of nature images, there might be a group of 20 images on each page, which download rapidly. The desired images can be

selected for viewing at a higher resolution. If all images appeared at full resolution, the page would take a long time to load.

TIFF (Tag/Tagged Image File Format)
A graphic image format widely used on the Internet.

time out, timed out, timeout
1 A message indicating that the time allotted to executing a request has ended, for example, when a request is sent to an Internet server and it does not answer after a specific time period.
2 When a user is disconnected from the Internet after a certain amount of time has elapsed. This usually occurs when the user does not perform any actions.

TLA (Three-Letter Acronym)
An acronym widely used on the Internet, especially in e-mail messages, *chats* and *newsgroups*. Although three-letter acronyms are the most common, there are also two-, four- or more letter acronyms. See ACRONYMS

TLD (Top-Level Domain)
See DOMAIN

tn3270
A special type of *Telnet* used to connect to mainframe IBM computers.

to:
In e-mail, the area that shows the addressee.

toolbar

A row of buttons located under the browser's menu bar which allows the user to perform the most frequent operations by clicking on the appropriate button, for example, go to the previously visited page, refresh the current page or access favourite sites.

Top-Level Domain
See DOMAIN

Torvald, Linus
See LINUX

traffic
1 The amount of information which travels through a communications system. When there is a lot of traffic, pages load slowly.
2 The number of visitors or accesses to a page or website. It can be measured in *hits* or *pageviews*.

traffic analysers
Programs which monitor the traffic generated on a website, how many visitors enter, how many pages they request and the most and least popular pages.

transfer rate
The rate at which data is sent or received over the Internet. It is measured in bits per second (bps).

translator
Software that allows the direct and quick translation of words on web pages.
There are various kinds, from those which can translate *chat* conversations immediately, thus allowing access to people

who do not speak the language used in that chat, to those which translate specific words on a web page or the whole page.

Transmission Control Protocol/Internet Protocol
See TCP/IP

transparent GIF
A *GIF* format that allows more aesthetic variations. Because one of the colours in the GIF format is transparent, when an image is located over a coloured background, it appears as if it were integrated in it. This allows for images with forms which are more pleasant than the typical rectangle.

Tripod

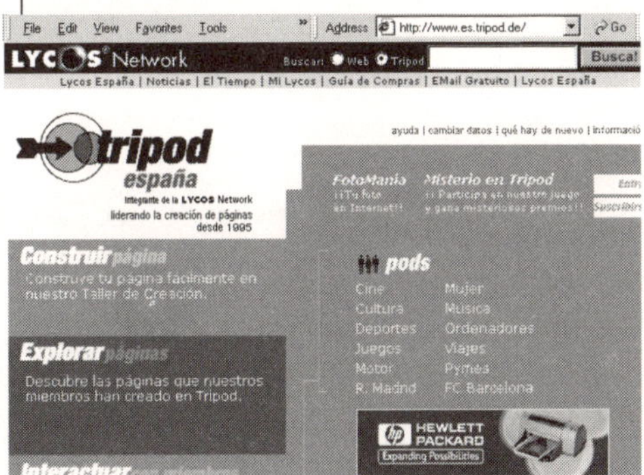

A company which owns an Internet website where users can create personal pages free of charge and put them up quickly on the Internet, allowing other users to access them. It is owned by *Lycos*. It can be visited at www.tripod.lycos.com

Trojan horse
A kind of computer virus. Its name comes from the siege of Troy by Greek troops, which lasted more than ten years. The seige ended when Ulysses signed an armistice with the Trojans and, as a goodwill gesture, gave them a gift of a huge wooden horse, which the Trojans brought into their city. However, there were Greek warriors hidden inside the horse who, under cover of darkness, crept out and opened the city's gates, allowing the Greek troops to enter and conquer Troy.
This kind of virus is likened to the mythical wooden horse because it takes on the appearance of a computer game or utility, when in reality its aim is to infect the computer. When the user plays the game or uses the application, the Trojan Horse deletes files from the system, and can even delete all information on the hard disk. There are cases in which they have been used to access computers and to read or modify files.
See VIRUS

troll
A message put up in a *newsgroup* with the sole objective of generating controversy and eliciting swift and inflamed responses. The best reaction to trolls is to ignore them.

TRUSTe
A website seal indicating a symbol of trust. The idea for this company began in March

1996 during a lecture by Esther Dyson in the PC Forum called 'Trust'. Two of the audience, Lori Fena (from the Electronic Frontier Foundation) and Charles Jennings (founder and CEO of Portland Software), met after the event. Both had the idea of creating a symbol of trust within the Internet, so they started a project.

In July 1996, EFF and CommerceNet announced a trial program for the worldwide launch of this initiative, in which 100 websites took part. TRUSTe was launched in June 1997, and continues to expand its number of companies, with presence today in all of the most outstanding *portals* and *e-commerce* companies.
Websites which include its seal follow the norms established by TRUSTe.
It can be visited at www.truste.org

UDP (User Datagram Protocol)
A protocol which is part of the *TCP/IP* protocol suite. It is used for data transfer with an enhanced reliability level.

UMTS (Universal Mobile Telecommunications System)
A new wide-band mobile telephone standard which allows Internet access at 2 Mbps.

uncompressing
The process of expanding a compressed archive so it recovers its original form. One of the best-known compressors for Windows is *WinZip*. Compression programs are widely used on the Internet to enable quicker file transfer. Also known as 'decompressing'.

under construction

A phrase seen on many Internet pages, although it is sometimes replaced by a graphic of a man at work. It indicates that

the page being accessed is not yet ready or maybe hasn't even been started. It is advisable to wait until the page is finished before displaying it, rather than leave this type of message on a website.

Uniform/Universal Resource Locator
See URL

UNIX
A multi-user (able to be used simultaneously by several individuals) and multitasking operating system invented in the late 1960s and early 1970s by AT&T, Bell Laboratories, GE and MIT.
It was used for developing the Internet communication protocols and is currently the most common operating system on Internet servers.

UNIX to UNIX Encode
See UUENCODE

unzip
To decompress archives, i.e. expand files which have been reduced in size using compression software which stores them in .zip format.
There are many programs which do this, such as PKZip, StuffIt Expander and *WinZip*.
See STUFF, ZIP

upload
To transmit data from one computer to another remote one on the Internet using a modem. For example, when web pages are updated via *FTP*, that information is uploaded to the computer where it is hosted. It is the opposite of *download*.

urban legend
A story on the Internet, usually invented or exaggerated, which spreads quickly, becoming a legend or a myth. The word comes from the Latin 'legenda', which means 'reading'. As in ther real world, Legends are events which are not based on historical fact. There are many of them on the Internet and there are even websites devoted to collecting and displaying them. They are usually spread through e-mail messages or *newsgroups*.

URL (Uniform Resource Locator)
The standard address format for every Internet resource within the *World Wide*

Web. It indicates where that resource is located.
The URL is usually shown (or can be keyed in order to find it) in the browser's upper-left box.
The first part of the URL indicates the protocol type, such as *HTTP* (http://), *FTP* (ftp:), *Gopher*, *Telnet* (telnet://) or *newsgroups* (news:).
Each web page has its own URL address, and there cannot be two identical addresses. For example, http://www.atkearney.com/press/january.htm could be the URL address where A.T. Kearney's January press stories are stored. Thus, 'http://' is the protocol indicating it refers to a page on the World Wide Web, 'atkearney' is the name of the company, '.com' indicates the server or domain '.com' indicates it is a company), '/press/' is the *path* and '/january.htm' denotes the specific page's file name within the website.

USENET, USENET Newsgroups, USENET News
An acronym from 'USEr NETwork'.
See NEWSGROUPS

user
An individual who uses a specific piece of computer software, such as an Internet browser. On the Internet, a 'registered user' is an individual who has passed his or her data to a specific website which might charge for access. The user is usually provided with a user ID and a password in order to access information.

User Datagram Protocol
See UDP

user ID, username
The unique alphanumeric identifier that must be typed every time access is required to a specific service on the Internet. The user ID is used along with a *password*.

UUDecode (UNIX to UNIX Decode)
See UUENCODE

UUEncode (UNIX to UNIX Encode)
A program used to convert a non-*ASCII* binary computer file (sound, video, im-

ages, etc.) into an ASCII document so that it can be transmitted as a text message via e-mail or in *newsgroups*. To return it to its original form, the person to whan the document was sent must reverse the process, or UUDecode it, with a decoding program. UUEncode is available as a UNIX command as well as in versions for MS-DOS and Apple Macintosh. However, most users are unaware of the existence of this program on their system, as most modern e-mail systems carry out this process automatically, without any intervention from the user.
See MIME, BinHex

VDOLive®
Software used to view video as it is being downloaded. The file can be viewed as soon as downloading begins; it is not necessary to wait until the complete file is downloaded.
See STREAM

VeriSign Inc.

VeriSign™

A company from California which is the leader in Internet authentication, validation and payments, services which are used by other websites, companies and *e-commerce* providers in order to carry out secure *e-commerce* transactions and communications over *IP* networks.

VeriSign Secure Site Click to verify

By mid-2000, the company had issued more than 210,000 digital *certificates* to websites and almost four million to individuals. It can be visited at www.verisign.com

Veronica (Very Easy Rodent Oriented Net-wide Index to Computerised Archives)
A tool which searches for information using keywords in a *Gopher* site's directories, files and documents. It is not widely used now, since faster and more capacious Internet search engines have swiftly replaced it.
See GOPHER, JUGHEAD, ARCHIE

vertical portal
See VORTAL

video files
Digitised files which store videos in electronic format. Among the best-known formats are .avi, .mpg, .qt (*QuickTime*) and .mov.

video conferencing, videoconference
Communication between two or more persons through a computer network, in which they can see images and listen to sounds. Videoconferencing enables conversations to be established with people in other geographic locations as if they were all in the same room. Special wideband telephone connections are required.
See CU-SEEME

viewer
A browser *plug-in* which enables the browser to manage files it could not recognise by itself, for example, to enable the user to watch or listen to some image, sound or video files. Viewers are also called 'helpers'.

The viewer operates outside the browser environment, but works alongside the program.

virtual
An adjective used for activities and objects within the Internet environment. It is referred to as a virtual environment or world, since it is not tangible; it can be seen and heard, but it comes from a computer environment.

virtual domain
See DOMAIN

virtual mall
See E-MALL

Virtual Private Network
See VPN

virtual reality (VR)
A three-dimensional (3D) environment created by a computer which simulates a real environment. In many cases, special headsets and gloves are needed to enhance the realistic effect.

virtual server
A section within the hard disk of a real server. For example, several websites can be hosted within one server, although each is accessed as if it were a dedicated web server.

virtual storefront
A shopfront similar to those in the real world, in which various products can be seen, chosen for inclusion in a *shopping cart*, paid for electronically and received later (or immediately, if they are digital products such as *MP3* music files, e-books, documents, etc.).

virus
A computer program, created to cause harm, which surreptitiously enters other computers, upsets their normal operation, and can destroy data, cancel functions, etc. As a general rule, the user will not know the virus is there until it starts executing its functions. These can be harmful or not, and viruses can either swiftly delete all information on the hard disk or act slowly. When the program or document in which the virus is hidden is opened, the virus is activated and begins its destructive work. If the document is sent to another person, the attached virus is also sent. Viruses can remain dormant for a long time before being activated. Some of them are activated on a specific day of the year, such as Friday the 13th.
To prevent viruses from entering a computer, an antivirus program should be installed. These can detect viruses and eliminate or prevent access to them. These programs must be constantly updated, since new viruses appear every day. McAfee VirusScan and Norton AntiVirus are the best-known programs.
On the Internet, the usual means of access for viruses are e-mail messages, to which files can be maliciously or unknowingly attached and sent, infecting other computers. Another access medium are infected floppy disks or CD-ROMs; viruses can even be downloaded when accessing specific files within a website, but not when browsing web pages or reading the text of an e-mail message, as

some people believe. There are hundreds of thousands of viruses in existence, with more being created all the time, and it is practically impossible to be completely protected against them.
Some of the most notorious Internet infections have been carried out in this fashion, as in the case of the 'I LOVE YOU' virus. The user received an e-mail message with these words as the title. When it was opened, the computer was automatically infected, and the virus used its e-mail system to send new messages to all the addressees in the infected user's address book. These messages, in turn, included the virus. Within a few days, it caused many e-mail servers belonging to large companies to crash, and the computers of tens of thousands of users to become infected.
See TROJAN HORSE

visit
To enter or browse a website.

visitor
An Internet user who enters a website and of whose entrance there is proof. The daily or monthly visitor number is the number of different individuals who have accessed a website that day or month. The visitor number measures access to the website, independent of the number of pages accessed by each visitor to the site. This term causes confusion, since the same visitor can enter on different days, counting as different visitors despite it being the same person.

vortal (vertical portal)
The name given to *portals* which are specific to a business sector and which store information relevant to it. For example, a portal for the construction sector, in which construction materials can be purchased, regulations can be checked, and users can participate in forums with other builders, etc., would be called a vortal.
'Portal' and 'vortal' are words with ill-defined boundaries. They can include all sites which include information and sales. When they belong to a specific sector, they are usually called vertical portals, and nowadays this term and 'vortal' are used interchangeably.
For more information on vertical portals or vortals, visit www.verticalnet.com, which collects a large amount of information on various vertical portals.

VPN (Virtual Private Network)
A private network connecting computers within a public network such as the Internet. It is a cheaper solution than the use of dedicated lines. Data confidentiality is guaranteed through the use of *encryption* systems in the communications.

VRML (Virtual Reality Modelling/ Markup Language)
A standard vector programing language created for building three-dimensional (3D) images on the Internet. For example, 3D worlds can be created in which *Internauts* can move and interact. Such is the case of virtual cities, commercial centres, *chat rooms* or Internet games.
Recent versions of browsers include VRML visualisers. In older ones, additional programs must be downloaded to view these files.

W3
An acronym of *World Wide Web.*

W3C (World Wide Web Consortium)

An international consortium founded in October 1994 that develops standards of common protocols that permit the World Wide Web to evolve and ensure its interoperativity. W3C is managed by the *MIT* (Massachusetts Institute of Technology) 'Laboratory for Computer Science' and was formerly established in the *CERN*, in Switzerland.
Its services include a repository with information for users and developers, prototypes and examples of applications using new technologies and reference codes to build and promote standards. Its site may be visited at www.w3.org

WAIS (Wide Area Information System/Service)
A search engine that tracks and indexes considerable amounts of information in servers through networks such as the Internet, showing the information to the person conducting the search. *Portal* search engines have shifted away from their original use, but this is still common in research and library environments and in other more academic areas where the results of a search are largely text based.

wallet
An electronic wallet or purse. It is software that is integrated with the browser to store and control the cards and *SET* certificates used in transactions on the Internet.
See SET

Walt Disney Internet Group
A company dedicated to Internet business belonging to the Walt Disney Company. It owns some of the most visited websites in the world, such as www.disney.com (for children and families), www.ESPN.com (for sports) and www.ABC.com. Other outstanding websites are www.family.com, www.movies.com, www.disneystore.com, www.disneytravel.com and www.NBA.com.
According to Media Matrix, in June 2000 it was the sixth most popular group on the Internet, with nearly 22 million visitors each month. Anothey key site is www.disney.go.com.

WAN (Wide Area Network)
A computer network that covers a geographical area bigger than a *LAN* territory, for example a network joining several cities.

WAP (Wireless Application Protocol)
Technology that enables the user to access the Internet with a cellular telephone or a WAP emulator. The contents of the sites must be adapted due to the smaller size, lower resolution and fewer colours

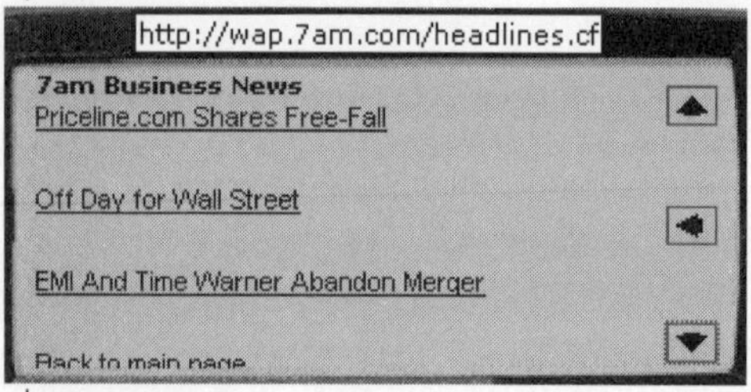

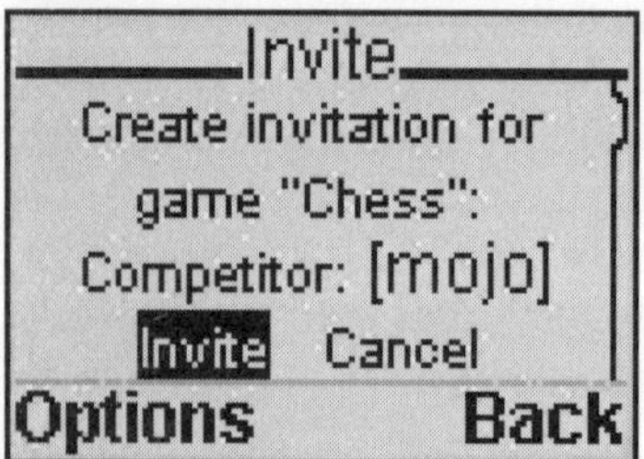

afforded by the telephone screen. This is a drawback, as it means that pages cannot be viewed as they are on a computer monitor.

WAP was developed by several technological companies, including Nokia, Ericsson, Motorola and Phone.com.

The language used for creating WAP contents is WML (Wireless Markup Language). See WML

WAP server

An HTTP server for the *WAP* environment.

.wav

A very common audio file extension.

Web

1 A term frequently used to refer to the *World Wide Web.* WWW and W3 are also used.

2 A website or place to find out information about a company, organisation or individual under a *domain* or subdomain. For example, A.T.Kearney's web may be found at www.atkearney.com

3 A web page, i.e. each individual page which forms part of a website.

web authoring

See AUTHORING

web browser

See BROWSER

web developer

A developer of advanced websites.

web document

An Internet document as it is viewed on a browser.

web host

See HOST, HOSTING

web page

See PAGE

web ring, webring

See RING

web server

A computer that provides web pages to its users.

website, web site, web presence, site
A group of related web pages that represent information about a company or individual on the Internet. There is usually a home page, from which access is gained to the rest of the pages, often grouped by category. A website may be stored on one or several servers.
Each page in a website has its own *URL* or 'http://' address.
An *FTP* site consists of directories to up- and download files, and a *Gopher* site is a group of menus.

web spider
See SPIDER

webcam, web camera, cam, live cam

A video camera connected to a computer that provides current images via a website. The images are reloaded after a fixed interval of a few seconds or minutes.
There are thousands of cameras that offer all kinds of images on the Internet. There are webcams that show the traffic in a city, the atmosphere in a nightclub, the weather in a certain area, monuments all around the world, offices, bird tables,

zoos, aquariums, private houses, etc. The examples show the elephants at the Pittsburgh zoo and a view of Rome.

webcasting
The delivery of live or pre-recorded audio or video to the user via the Web. It is frequently used to send film trailers, video clips, or radio or television programmes. It uses the *push* technology, where the server sends continuous information to the user, where the user has previously requested this information.

Webcrawler

WEBCRAWLER™ "It's that Simple."

Owned by Excite, one of the main search engines on the Internet. Find it at www.webcrawler.com

webmail
A mail delivery service offered from a web page; it is generally free and is very common in *portals*.

webmaster

The administrator, usually with HTML expertise, responsible for a website's performance. In many cases, he or she is also the creator of the website's contents and organisation. The term is very broad and may cover other responsibilities, such as web-server administration. If the webmaster is a woman, the term 'webmistress' is often used.
The webmaster/mistress can usually be accessed by e-mail at webmaster@company-name.com.

WebNFS

A product of *Sun Microsystems* put forward as a standard that extends its NFS (Network File System) to the Internet.
See NFS

WebTV

Microsoft webtv

A company founded in 1995 and taken over in 1997 by Microsoft for 425 million dollars. It was created in a car-dealer's

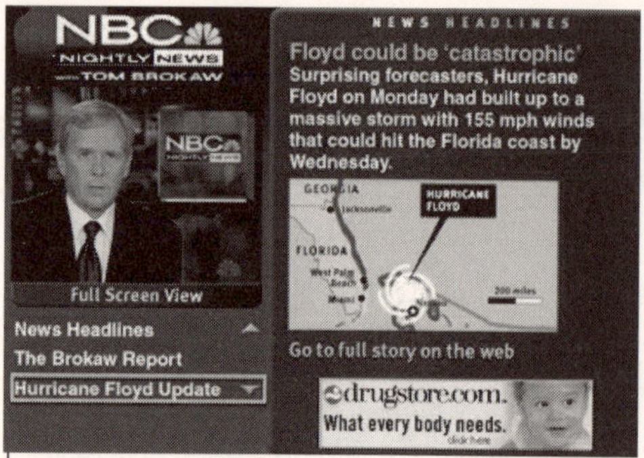

garage in Palo Alto, California. It allows access to the Internet through television, also adding interactive facilities to the television programming itself.
A *set-top box* is needed, including a modem, an optional keyboard, browsing software, and the availability of a telephone line. Visit its website at www.webtv.net

White Pages

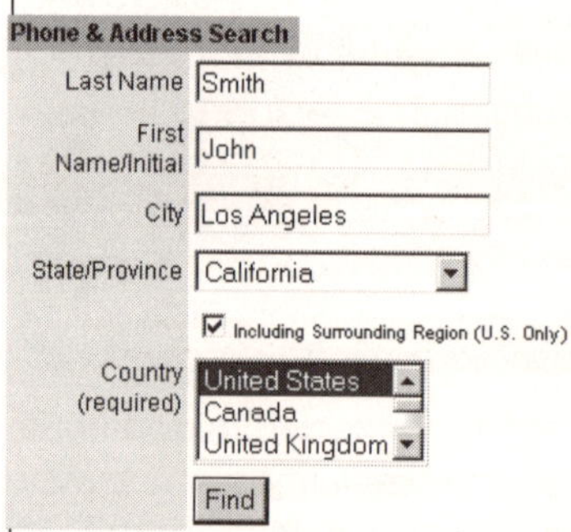

The name, taken from real-world telephone directories, occasionally given to an Internet directory offering e-mail addresses, telephone numbers and mail addresses of Internet users. The example shows the White Pages of the *MSN portal*.
See YELLOW PAGES

white paper
A document created by a company that develops new technology explaining all the issues related to this technology, generally from a more technical point of view. For example, 'CD-ROM white paper'.

Whois

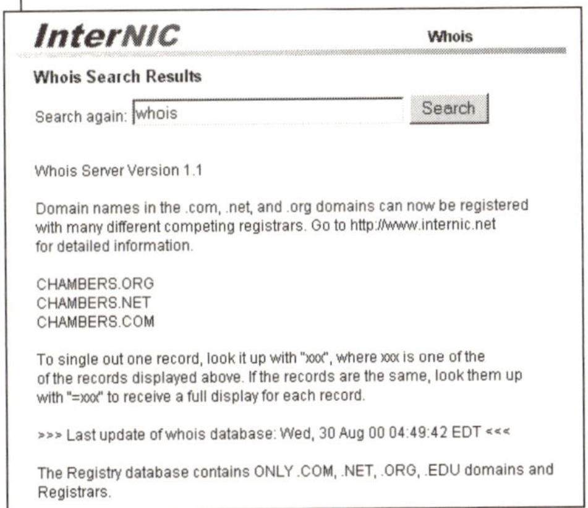
InterNIC **Whois**

Whois Search Results

Search again: whois Search

Whois Server Version 1.1

Domain names in the .com, .net, and .org domains can now be registered with many different competing registrars. Go to http://www.internic.net for detailed information.

CHAMBERS.ORG
CHAMBERS.NET
CHAMBERS.COM

To single out one record, look it up with "xxx", where xxx is one of the of the records displayed above. If the records are the same, look them up with "=xxx" to receive a full display for each record.

>>> Last update of whois database: Wed, 30 Aug 00 04:49:42 EDT <<<

The Registry database contains ONLY .COM, .NET, .ORG, .EDU domains and Registrars.

An *InterNIC* database that allows users to obtain information about Internet *domains* and hosts. Users can also find out if a domain they wish to register has already been registered and is therefore occupied, and look up data about the individual or company owning them, including the name, e-mail address, postal address and telephone number. If the database shows that the domain has not been registered and is free, it can be registered.
Apart from the InterNIC, this facility can also be found on other servers.
The above example shows the result of a search for the term 'chambers', where there are three corresponding domain registrations.

Wide Area Information System/ Service
See WAIS

Wide Area Network
See WAN

Winamp

One of the most commonly used pieces of software, it is used to play *MP3* files. It can be downloaded from www.winamp.com or www.mp3.com.

Windows sockets
See WINSOCKS

Winsock applications
Programs designed to use *Winsocks*.
See WINSOCKS

Winsocks (Windows Sockets)
DLL (Dynamic Link Library) programs from Microsoft Windows that allow programers to link (interface) with *TCP/IP* applications. They are the link that controls the relationship between a Windows program and another TCP/IP.

WinZip
A program from the Windows environment used to compress and store files in a smaller amount of disk space or to send

them more quickly over the Internet. It is a *shareware* program that can be downloaded from www.winzip.com.

Wired

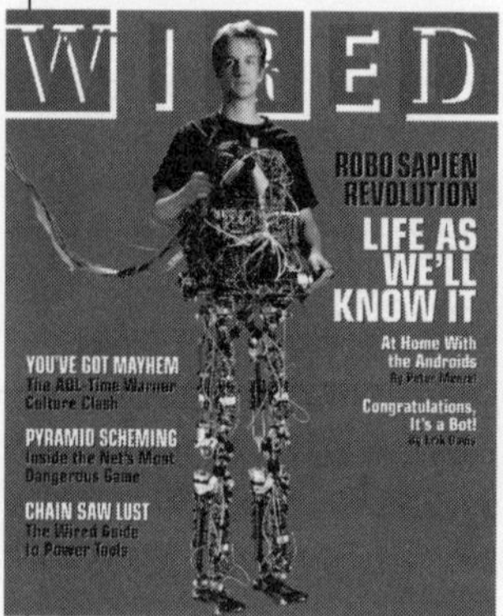

One of the most popular magazines in the Internet environment.
Visit its website at www.wired.com

wireless
Communication without wires, as with, for example, mobile phones, satellites or infrared signals.

Wireless Application Protocol
See WAP

WML (Wireless Markup Language)
A language similar to the *HTML* language, based in *XML*. Used in *WAP* devices by means of a special *browser*.
See WAP

World Wide Web, WWW, W3
An all-encompassing term used to refer to all the resources which can be accessed using services such as *Gopher*, *FTP*, *Telnet*, *USENET*, *WAIS* and others. However, it is most commonly associated with the *HTTP* server network that can combine text, graphics, audio and other formats in one document. This network is based on HTTP (HyperText Transfer Protocol), and the protocols are interrelated by means of hypertext links, which allow the user to go from one page to another one very easily. Thus, all pages form a 'web', linking the contents of all the pages on the Internet. Access to these pages and other services offered by the Internet is achieved using a *browser*, such as Microsoft *Explorer*, *Mosaic*, *Netscape* Communicator or *Opera*.
The Web and the Internet are two different things, although the terms are sometines used interchangeably.

World Wide Web Consortium
See W3C

worm
A computer programme created with a destructive purpose that can self-duplicate and self-disseminate. The most widely known is the 'Internet Worm', created in the late 1980s, that affected hundreds of servers, leaving them out of service.
See VIRUS

XHTML 1.0

The recommendation of the *W3C* for the *HTML* version after 4.01. It is a reformulation of HTML 4.01 in *XML*, combining the strength of the former and the power of the latter. It allows the creation of web pages for all browsing platforms, including the new ones, such as television, incar systems, cyberkiosks and mobile phones.

Xmodem

The standard protocol for transferring files via modem developed by Ward Christensen in 1997. It sends data in 128-byte blocks between PCs. The data incorporates a system that allows errors to be detected and verifies that data were not lost or damaged when the message arrives. If the message arrives intact, an *ACK* (acknowledgement) message is sent. If any data loss occurs, a *NAK* (negative acknowledgement) message is sent requesting retransmission.

Ymodem and *Zmodem* use bigger data blocks than Xmodem and are faster.
See Ymodem, Zmodem, ACK, NAK

XML (eXtensible Markup Language)

A universal language for marking up structured documents and data on the Web that is richer, more extensive and more dynamic than *HTML*. It is not only a markup language, but also a metalanguage that can describe other markup languages. It allows a non-limited use of the kinds of data that can be used on the Internet, thus solving the problems that existed between organisations needing to exchange data using different standards.
It originates from *SGML*, just as HTML does. Compared to HTML, it offers more possibilities for linking, better presentation and better browser facilities, and it is more accessible and reusable.
It is standard in the *W3C*. See the website at www.xml.com

Ya.com

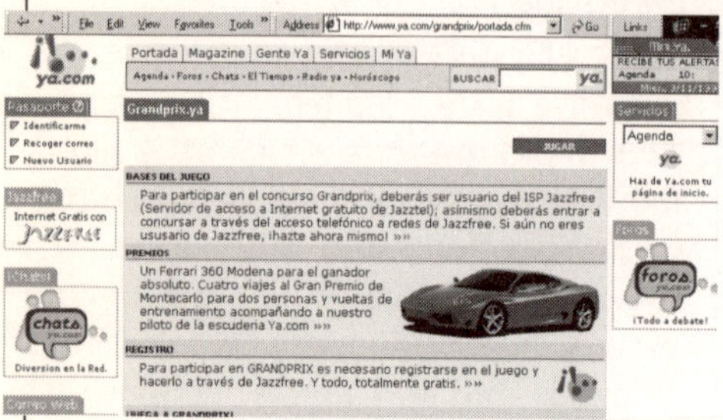

A *portal* owned by Jazztel, launched in 1999 for the Spanish market.
Its website is at www.ya.com

Yahoo!

YAHOO!

One of the best-known directories and *portals* in the Internet, created in 1994 by David Filo and Jerry Yang when they were Electrical Engineering students at Stanford University. They started creating a guide as a way to keep track of their personal interests on the Internet. Before long, they found that their home-brewed lists were becoming too long and unwieldy. Gradually, they began to spend more and more time on Yahoo! During 1994, they converted Yahoo! into a customised database, designed to serve the needs of the thousands of users who began to use the service through the closely bound Internet community. They developed customised software to help them efficiently locate, identify and edit material stored on the Internet.
The name Yahoo! is supposed to stand for 'Yet Another Hierarchical Officious Oracle', but its creators insist that they named it Yahoo! because they considered themselves yahoos (i.e. louts, hooligans).
Yahoo! itself first resided on Yang's student workstation, 'akebono', while the search engine was lodged on Filo's computer, 'konishiki'. (These machines were named after legendary Hawaiian sumo wrestlers.) In 1995, Marc Andreessen, co-founder of *Netscape* Communications, invited the Yahoo! creators to move their files over to the company's powerful computers.
By mid-2000, Yahoo! was being visited by more than 156 million people each month and had local versions in numerous other countries.
Its website is at www.yahoo.com

Yellow Pages (YP)

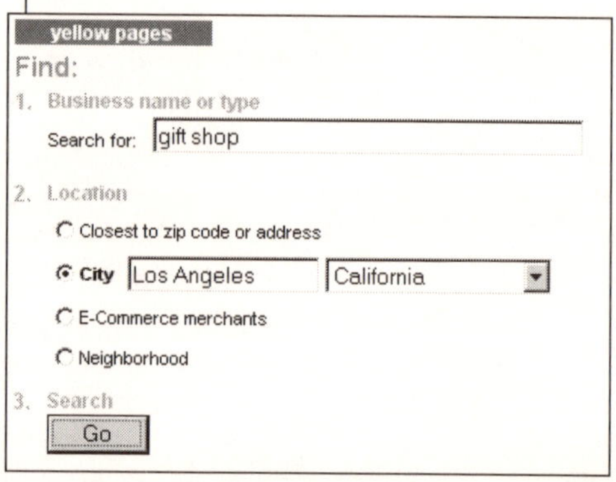

An Internet version of the standard telephone directory of services. The example shows a search in the Yellow Pages of the MSN *portal*.
See WHITE PAGES

Ymodem
A transfer protocol for modem based on the *Xmodem* that sends data from an Internet host to a personal computer. The data blocks occupy 1,024 bytes (compared to 128 bytes in the Xmodem), so transmission is faster. Correct data does not generate an *ACK* (acknowledgement) message confirming the reception of the information.
However, if data arrives with errors, a *NAK* (negative acknowledgement) message is sent to prompt retransmission. It allows the transmission of multiple files in one session.
See XMODEM, ZMODEM

zine
See E-ZINE

zip
A file-compression format used to store one or several documents in less space. There are several formats that can be used to perform this task; the most common are zip (the most widely used), TAR, gzip and CAB. Formats like ARJ, ARC and LZH are less common.
When large documents are sent by e-mail, it is advisable to convert them to zip format or similar so they can be sent and received in less time. Another advantage is that compressed files occupy less hard disk space. Documents compressed in this manner have the extension '.zip' after the file name, and they must be unzipped at the other end for the recipient to see the original documents.
The most widely used programs are PKZip (DOS environment) and *WinZip* (for Windows).
See STUFF, UNZIP

Zmodem
A fast transfer protocol for modem that sends the data from an Internet host to a personal computer. Multiple files can be sent with a single command, and the file names are sent together. Data is sent in blocks of 1,024 bytes. If a data block arrives with errors, a *NAK* (negative acknowledgement) is returned and the block is resent. It also has the ability to recover a partially performed transfer.

Zulu time
A term for the time according to Greenwich Mean Time (GMT), commonly used by the United States government.